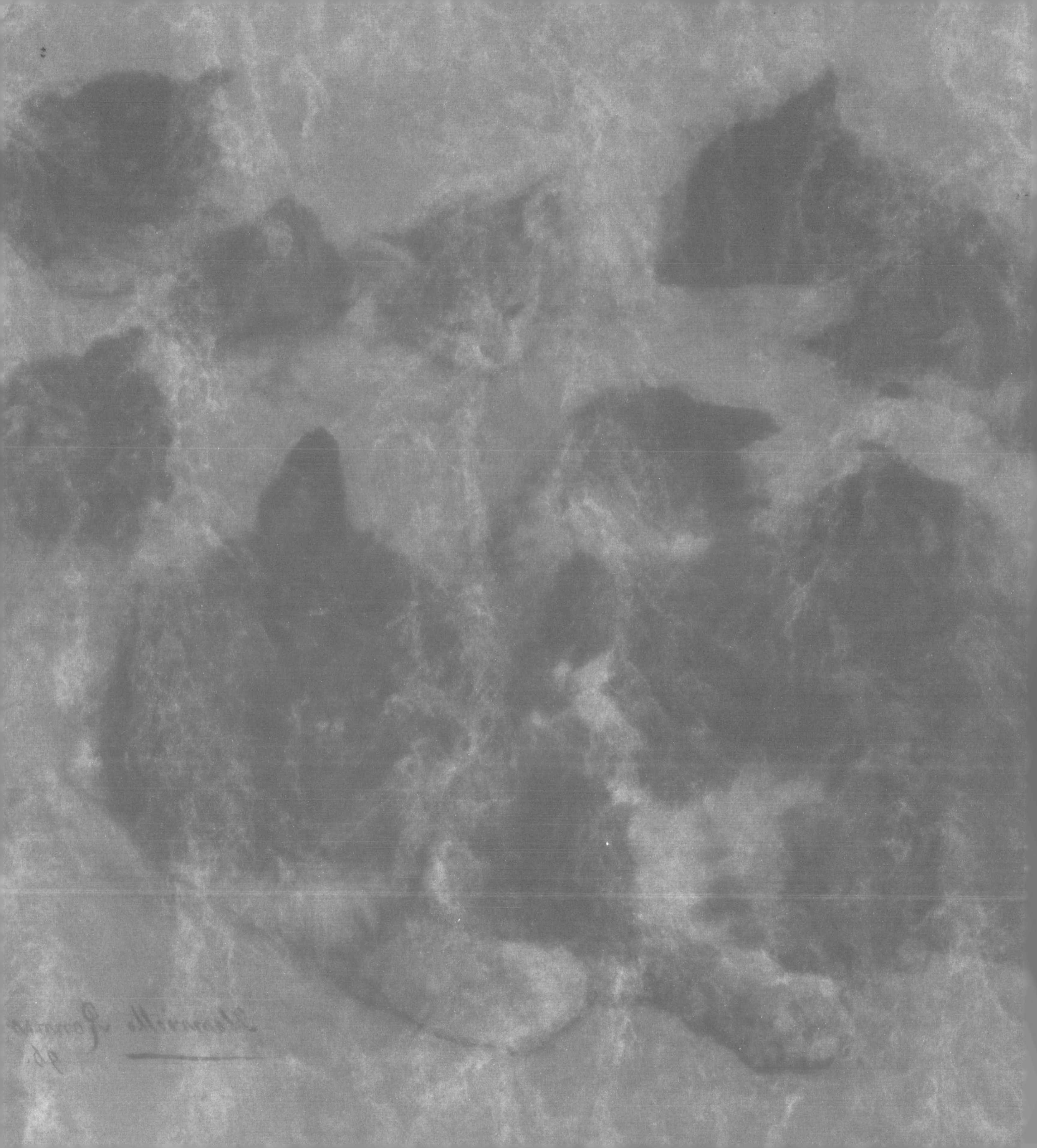

images of

THE CAT

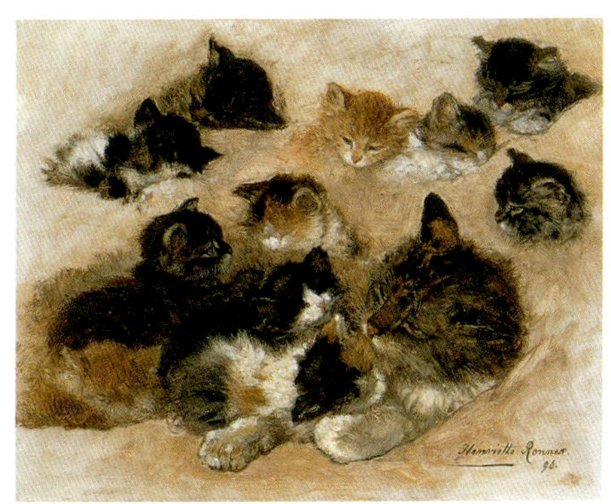

First published in 1999 by Hamlyn an imprint of Octopus Publishing Group Limited, 2-4 Heron Quays, London E14 4JP

Publishing Director Laura Bamford
Executive Editor Mike Evans
Editor Humaira Husain

Creative Director Keith Martin
Executive Art Editor Geoff Borin
Designer Louise Griffiths

Picture Research Zoë Holtermann
Production Controller Joanna Walker

A catalogue record for this book is available from the British Library

ISBN 0 600 59838 1

Produced by Toppan Printing Co Ltd

Printed in China

HAMLYN

images of
THE CAT

NIGEL CAWTHORNE

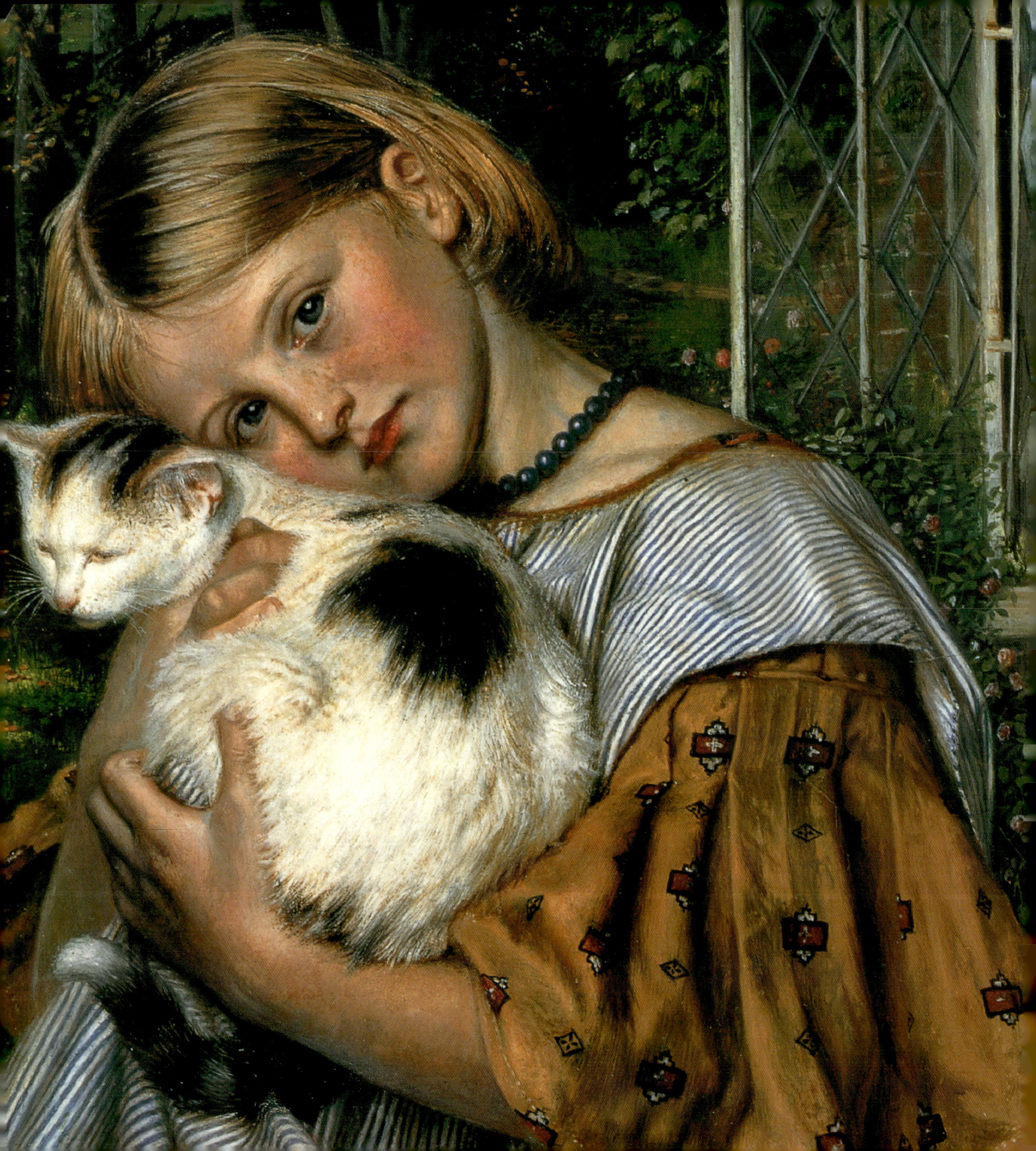

contents

1

ancestral cats

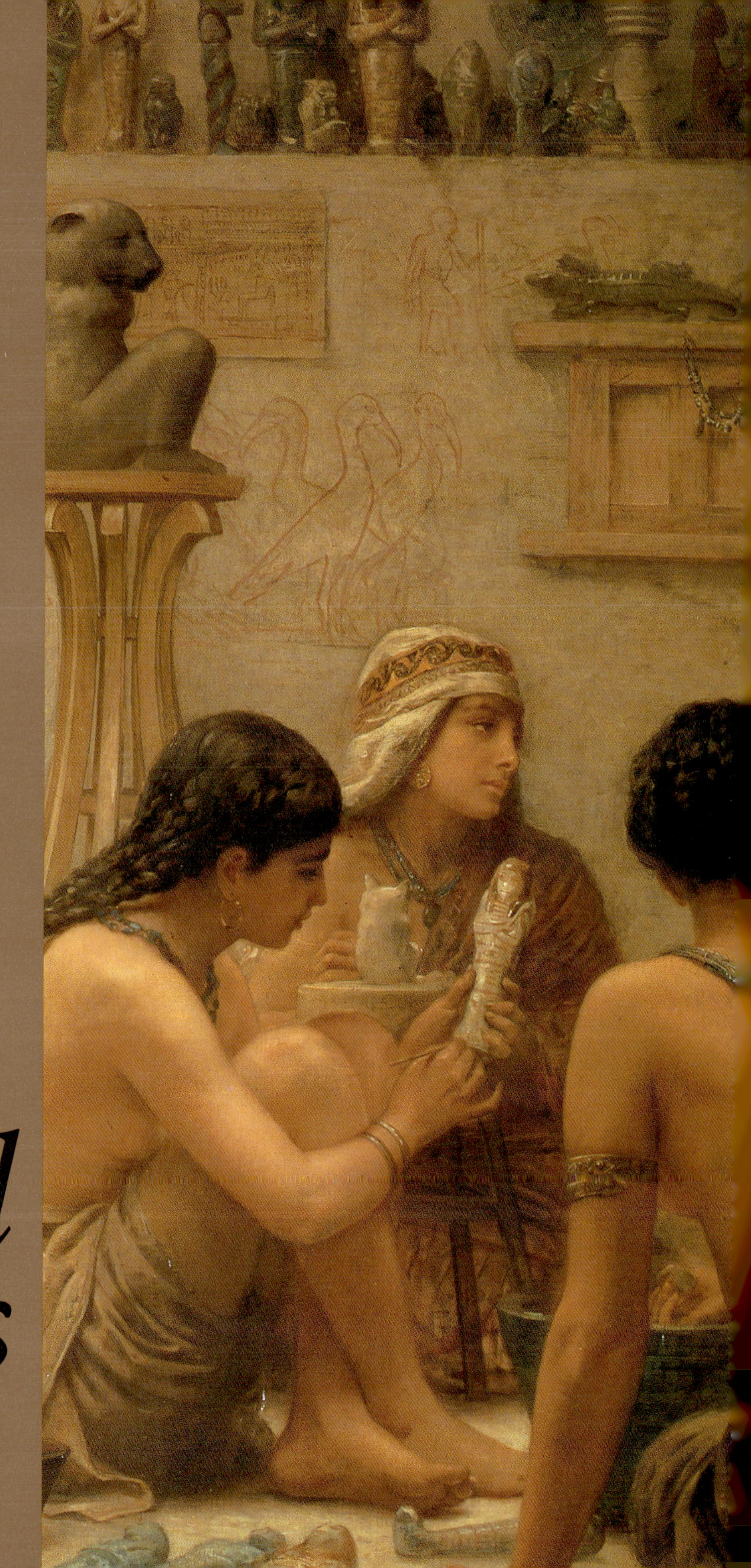

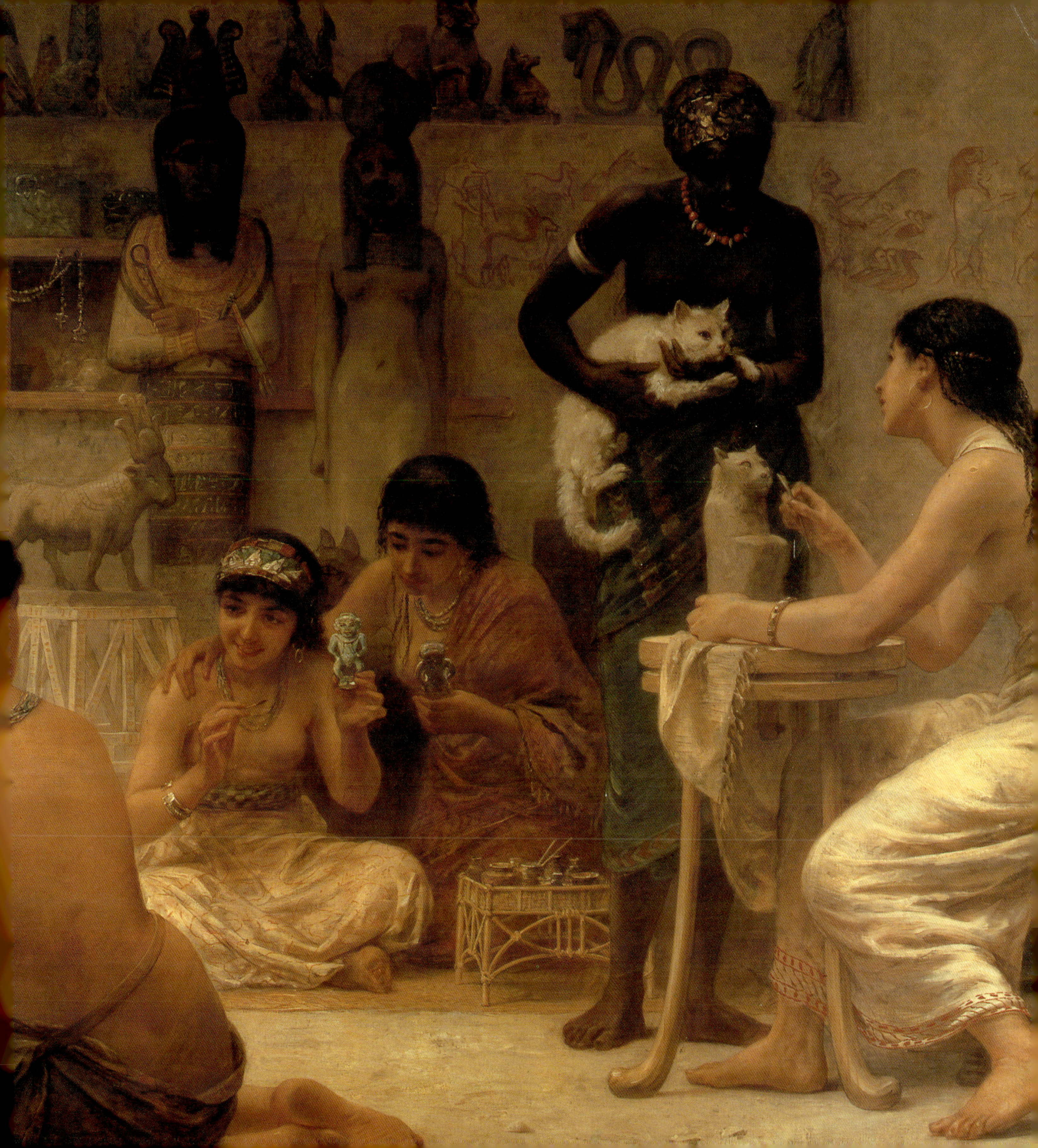

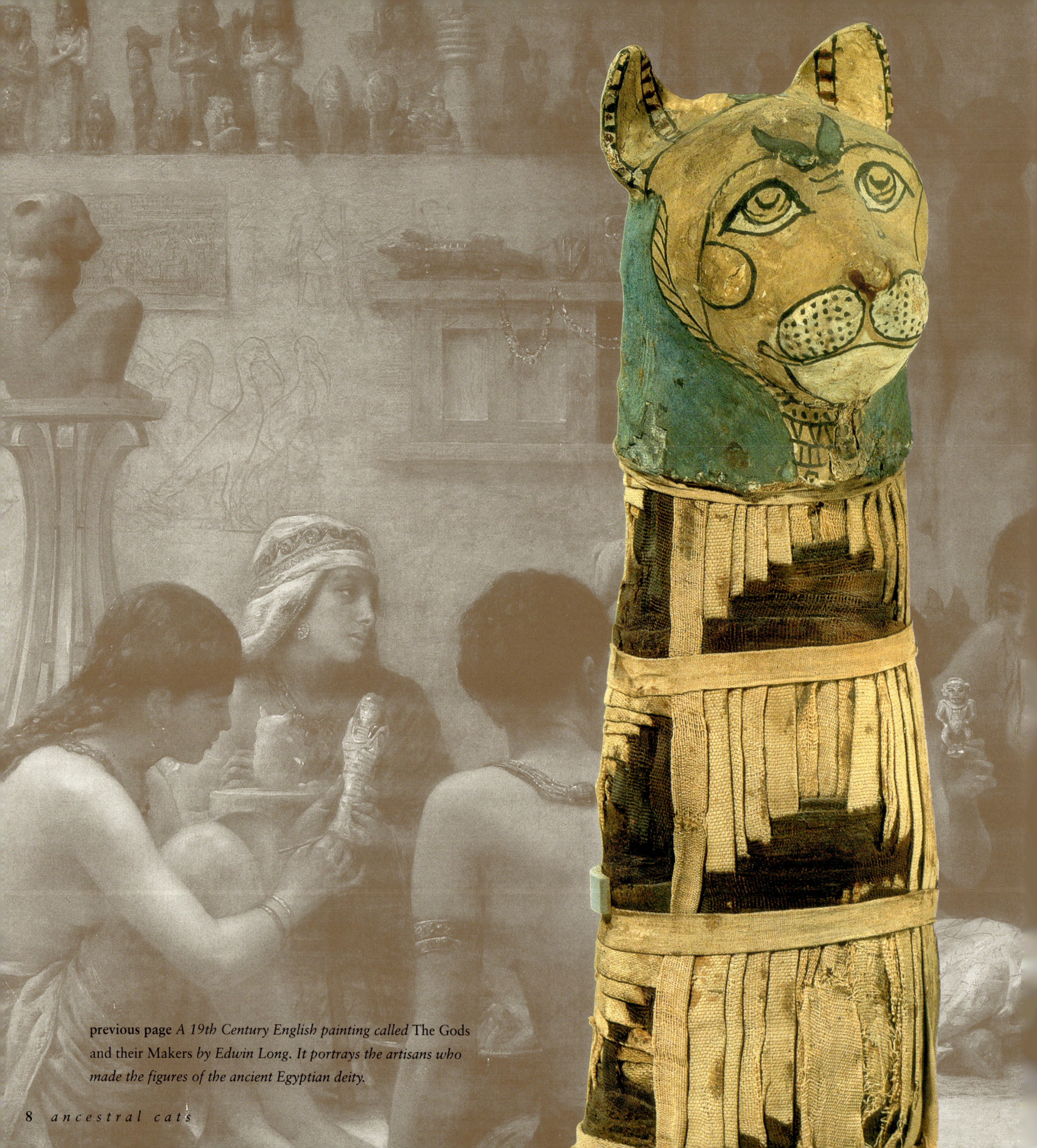

previous page *A 19th Century English painting called* The Gods and their Makers *by Edwin Long. It portrays the artisans who made the figures of the ancient Egyptian deity.*

left *An Egyptian mummified cat, stuccoed and painted, from the Late period, 664-332BC.*

Scientists believe that the cat's ancient ancestor was a weasel-like creature called the Miacis that lived some 55 million years ago. This extraordinary creature is also credited with being the ancestor of foxes, wolves, dogs, bears, racoons and the sabre-tooth tiger.

The cat as we know it today evolved around 10 million years ago when wildcats roamed Africa and Europe. They seem to have become domesticated in the Stone Age.

They were certainly a close companion of man in the earliest civilizations in ancient Sumeria. The proverb 'a cat for its thoughts, a mongoose for its actions' originated there between 2600 and 2400 BC. They were also known in India around that time. In the third millennium BC, in Chanhu-Daro in Sind, a dog chased a cat over a soft unbaked brick and the imprints of their paws have been preserved.

By the rise of the civilization in Egypt over 4,000 years ago, cats were revered. When they died, they were mummified like pharaohs and buried in their own pet cemetaries. In an ancient tomb in Thebes, there is a painting of a cat called Bouhaki. It is wearing gold earrings.

Hundreds of mummfied cats in their own elaborate coffins have been found in subterranean tombs in Bast temples, some surrounded by mummified mice so that they would have enough food – and entertainment – in the afterlife.

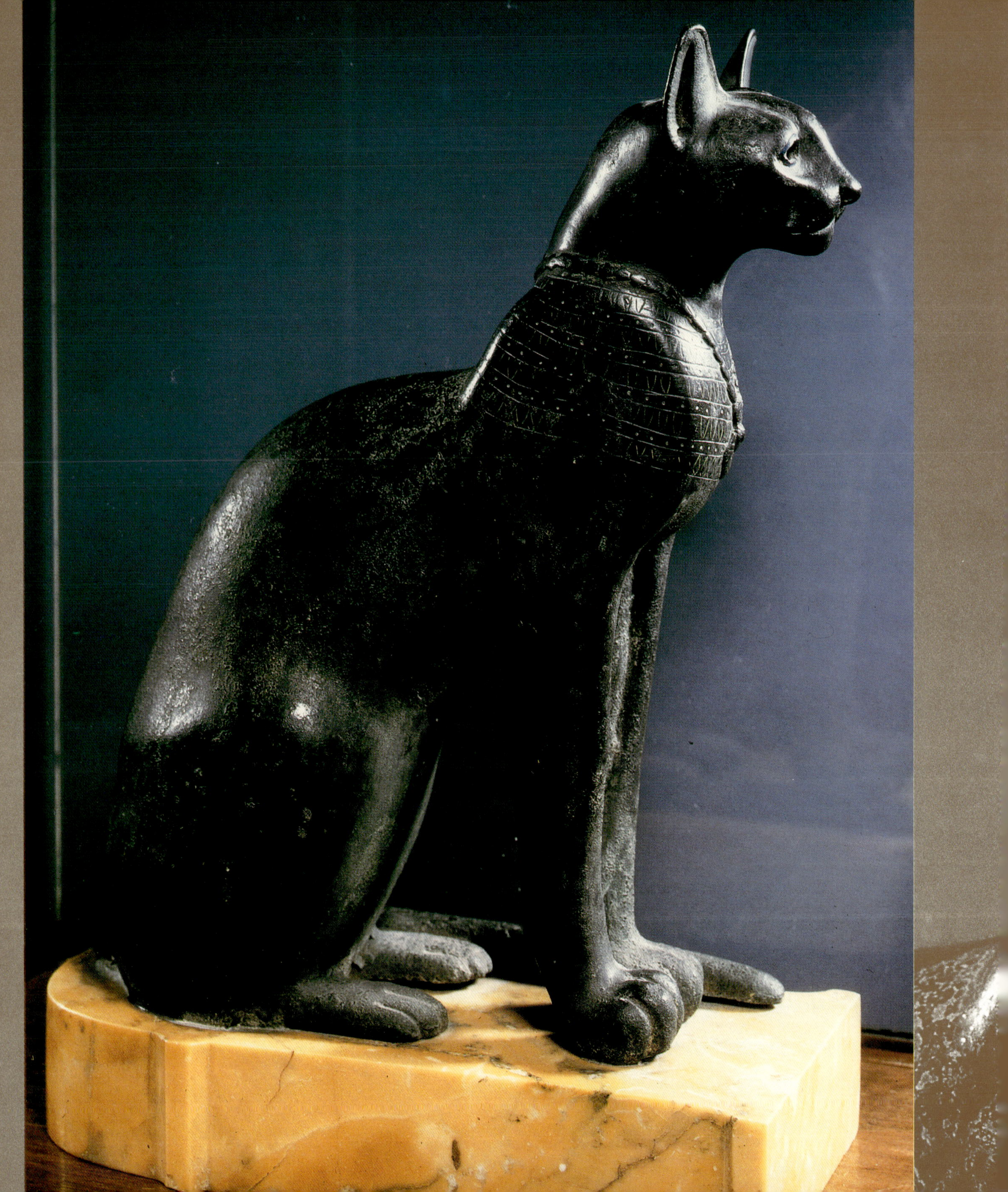

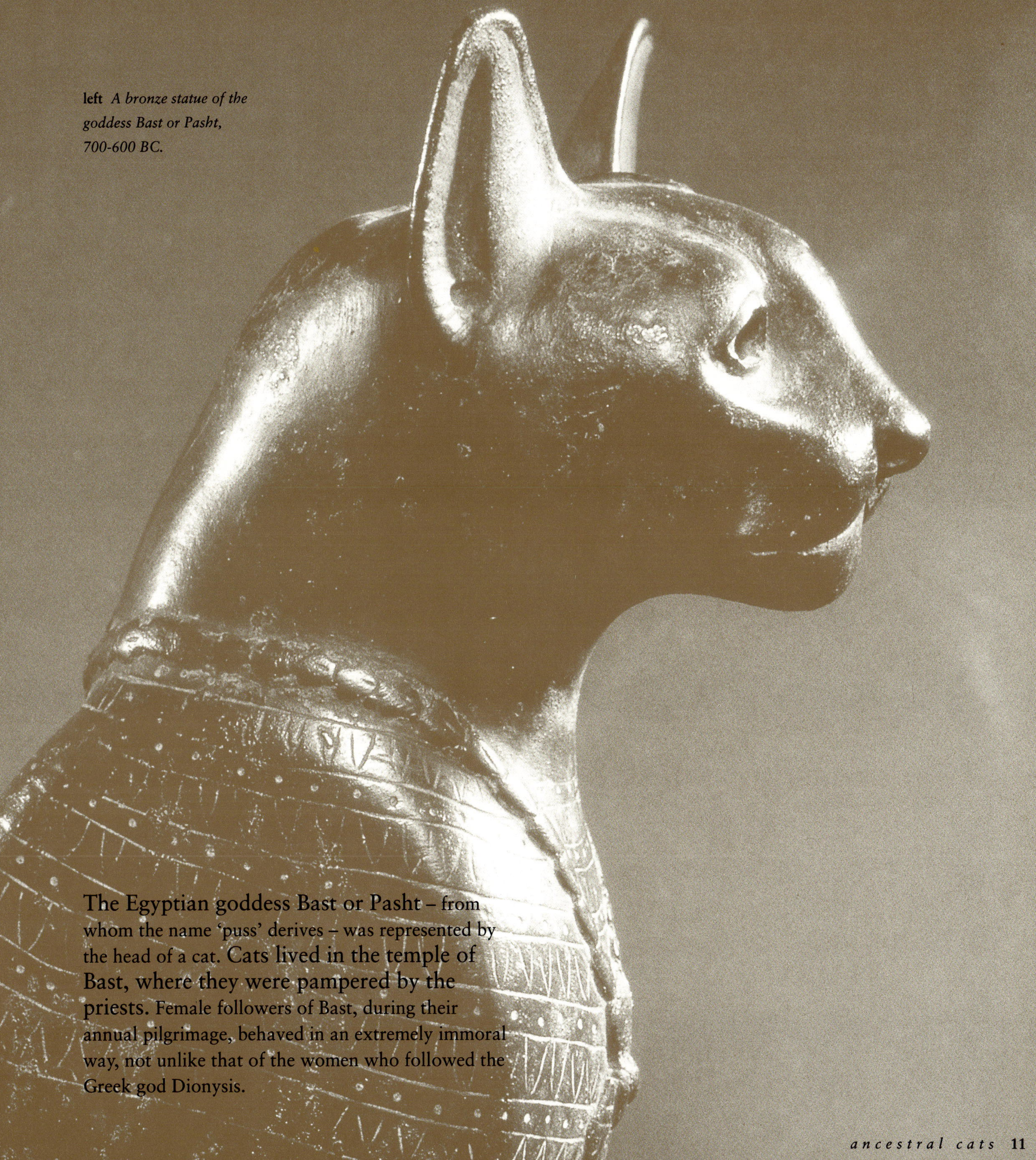

left *A bronze statue of the goddess Bast or Pasht, 700-600 BC.*

The Egyptian goddess Bast or Pasht – from whom the name 'puss' derives – was represented by the head of a cat. Cats lived in the temple of Bast, where they were pampered by the priests. Female followers of Bast, during their annual pilgrimage, behaved in an extremely immoral way, not unlike that of the women who followed the Greek god Dionysis.

In Japan, the Emperor found a litter of five kittens in the corner of his palace in Kyoto on the tenth day of the fifth moon of the year 999 (AD 339 in the Christian calendar). This was considered a time of great spirituality and he decreed that cats were to be considered semi-sacred. However, when silk production in Japan was threatened by mice, cats could not be employed to protect them because of the imperial degree. Statues of cats had to be used instead. These did not work. Eventually, to save the silk trade, the decree had to be rescinded. But it took over two hundred years.

In Tokyo, there is a temple dedicated to cats named Go-To-Ku-Ji. The Shinto deity, Maneki-neko, is represented as a cat with his forepaw raised. According to a Japanese legend, a nobleman was riding through a forest when he was stopped by a cat with its forepaw raised. Intrigued, the rider followed the cat who led him to a monastry where the monks were starving. He ordered his retinue to bring the monks food. They saw to it that the cat never went hungry again and when he died, they made an effigy as a symbol of good luck.

The Japanese also have an ogress Neko-Baké who takes the form of a cat. She creeps into the homes of disobedient children at night, steals them away and eats them.

right *A Japanese woodblock print from 1845, by Kuniyoshi* – Girl Chastising a Thieving Cat.

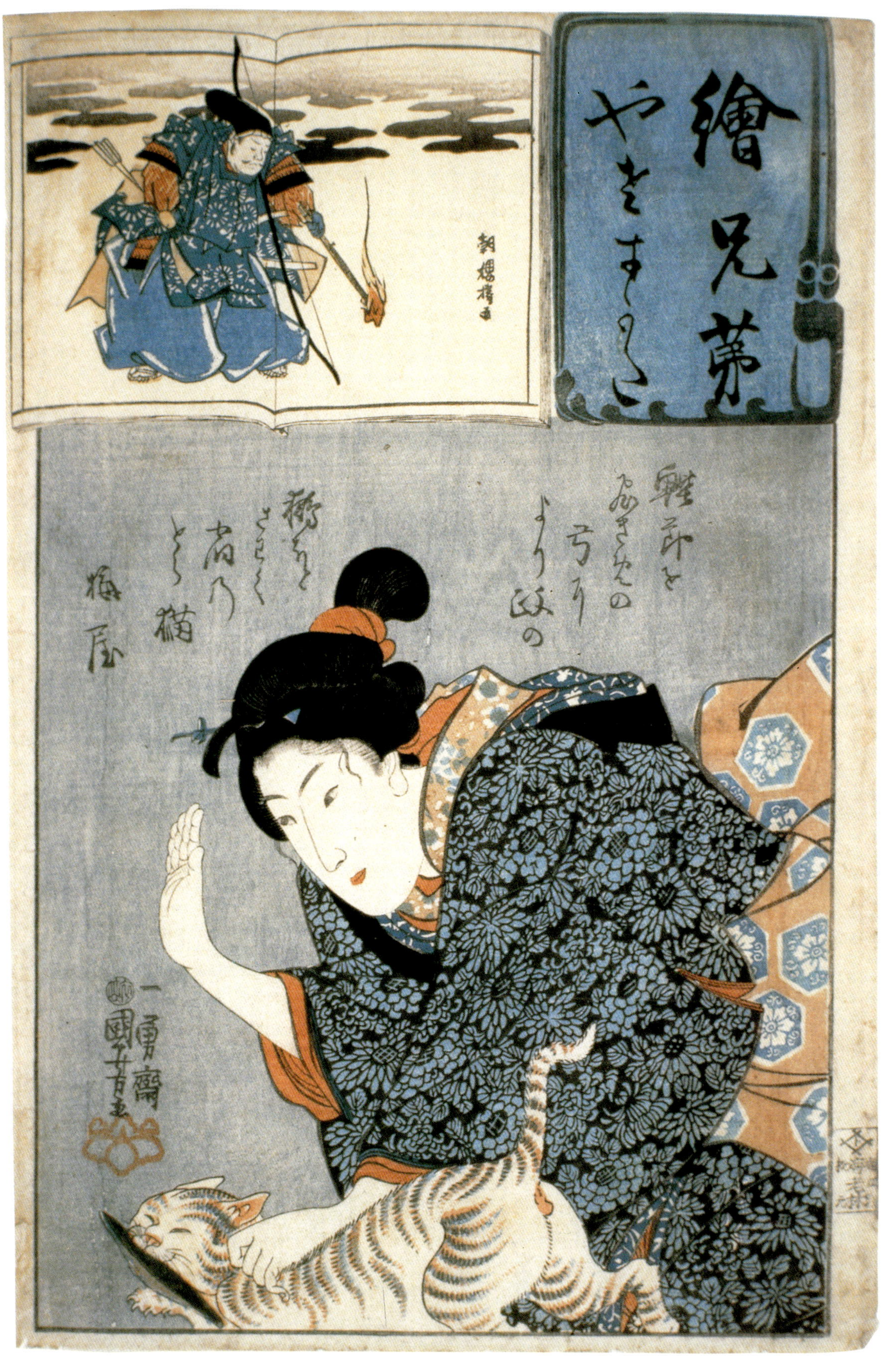
繪兄弟
一勇齋國芳画

According to legend, cats originated on Noah's ark. When Noah was troubled with mice and rats eating the stores of grain, he went to the lion for advice. The lion squeezed and brought forth a cat out of its nostril. This story contradicts folk lore on the Isle of Man which maintains that the Manx cat lost its tail because, distracted by a mouse, it was late boarding the ark and the door slammed shut severing the appendage. In fact, there are no mention of cats in the Bible. This may have been because of the deep suspicion the Israelites had of anything Egyptian. But cats often appear in religious paintings from the Renaissance, especially those depicting the Last Supper.

right *A High Renaissance depiction of the last supper by Francesco Bassano.*

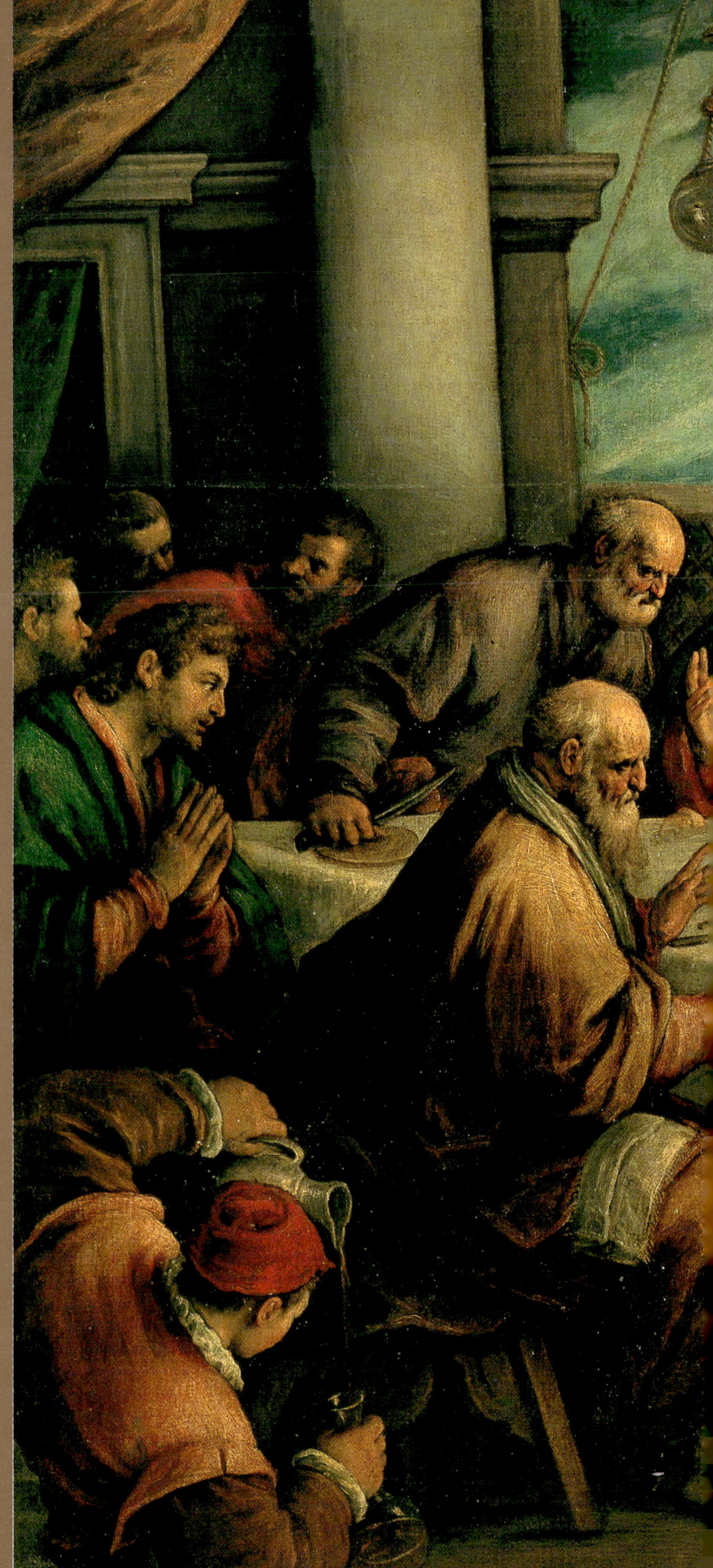

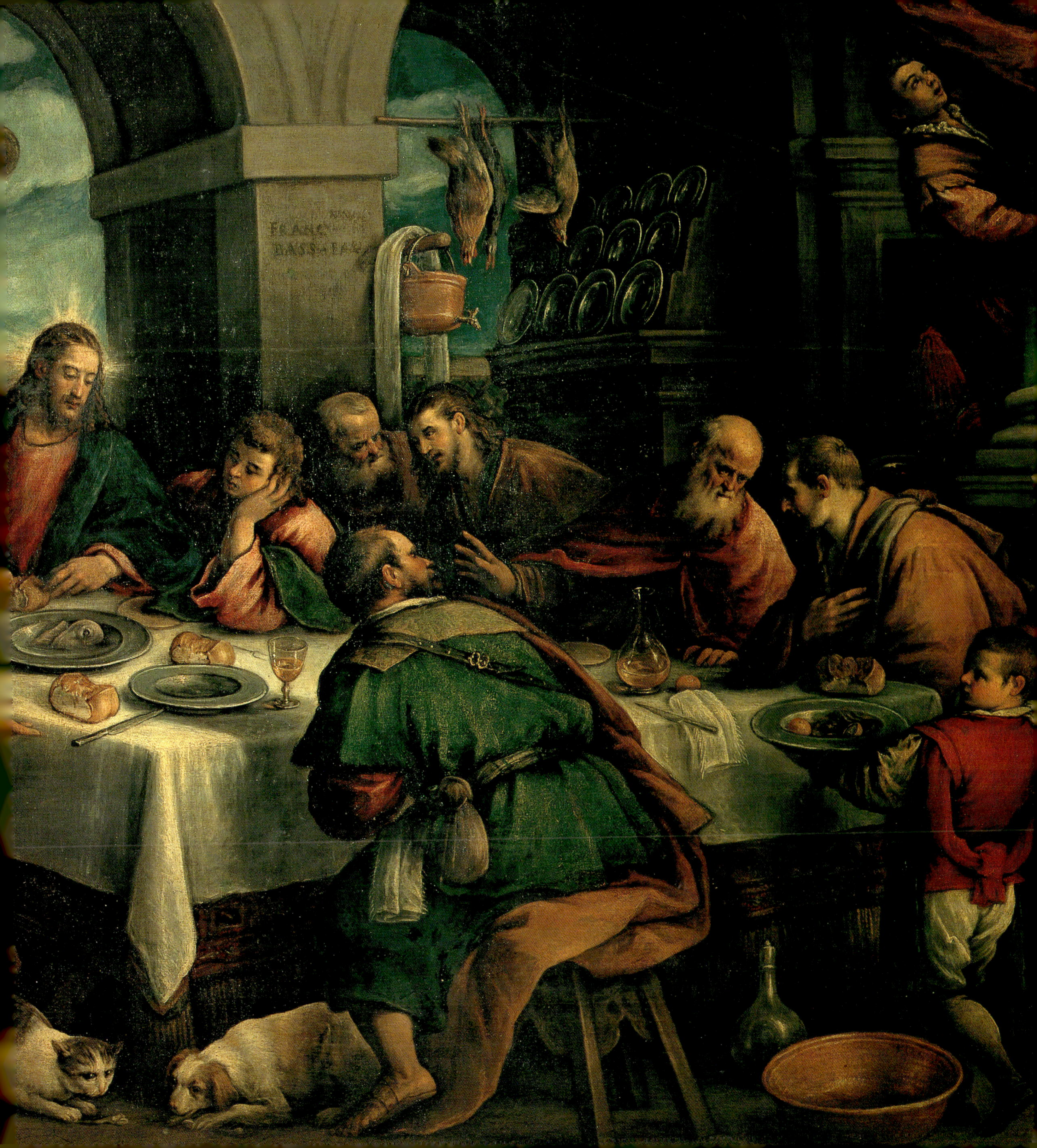

تنجوا السفينة فلما عرف السنور مقالة الجرذ عرف انه صادق فقال له ان
لك هذا الشبيه بالحق وانا ايضا راغب فيما ارجو الك ولنفسي به الخلاص ثم انك
ان فعلت ذلك ساشكرك ما بقيت قال الجرذ فاني سادنوا منك فاقطع

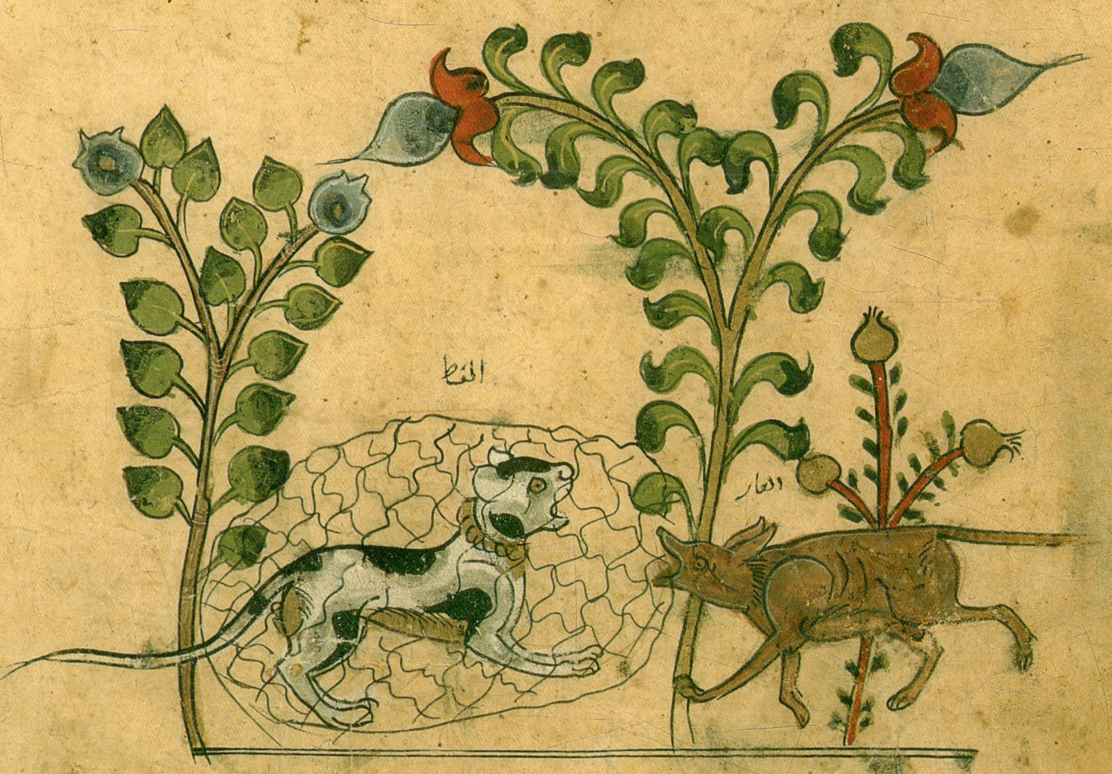

الحبايل كلها الا حبلا واحدا ابقيه لاستوثق لنفسي منك ثم اخذ في قرض حبايله ٥
ثم ان البوم وابن عرس لما رايا دنو الجرذ من السنور ايسا منه وانصرفا ثم ان
الجرذ ابطا على السنور في قطع الحبايل فقال له ما لي لا اراك مجدا في قطع حبايلي

ولكن هذا أشبه بالحمق وإنا انصار اعب فيما ارجو لك ولنفسي به السلامة ثم إنك

ان يعلمك ذلك سأذكر لك ما تعجب قال الجرذ فإني سأذنبوا منك فاقطع

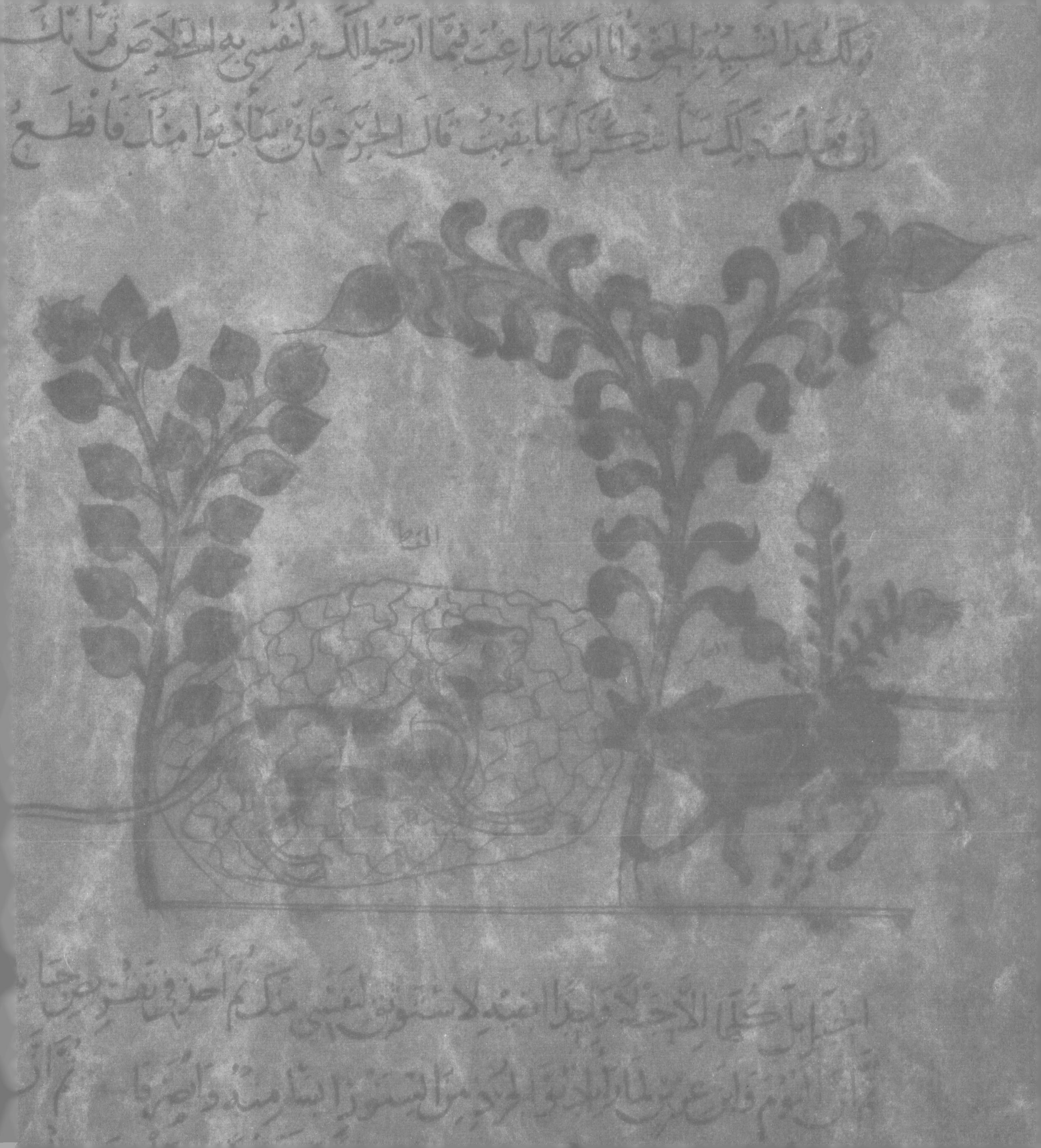

احبالك كلها الآخرة لكى ابدا تنبه لا تستوي لنفسي منكم احد في بعض حبالها

ثم ان اليوم ولن غير هذا الا الجرذ من التسوية ابتدا منه واصرخ

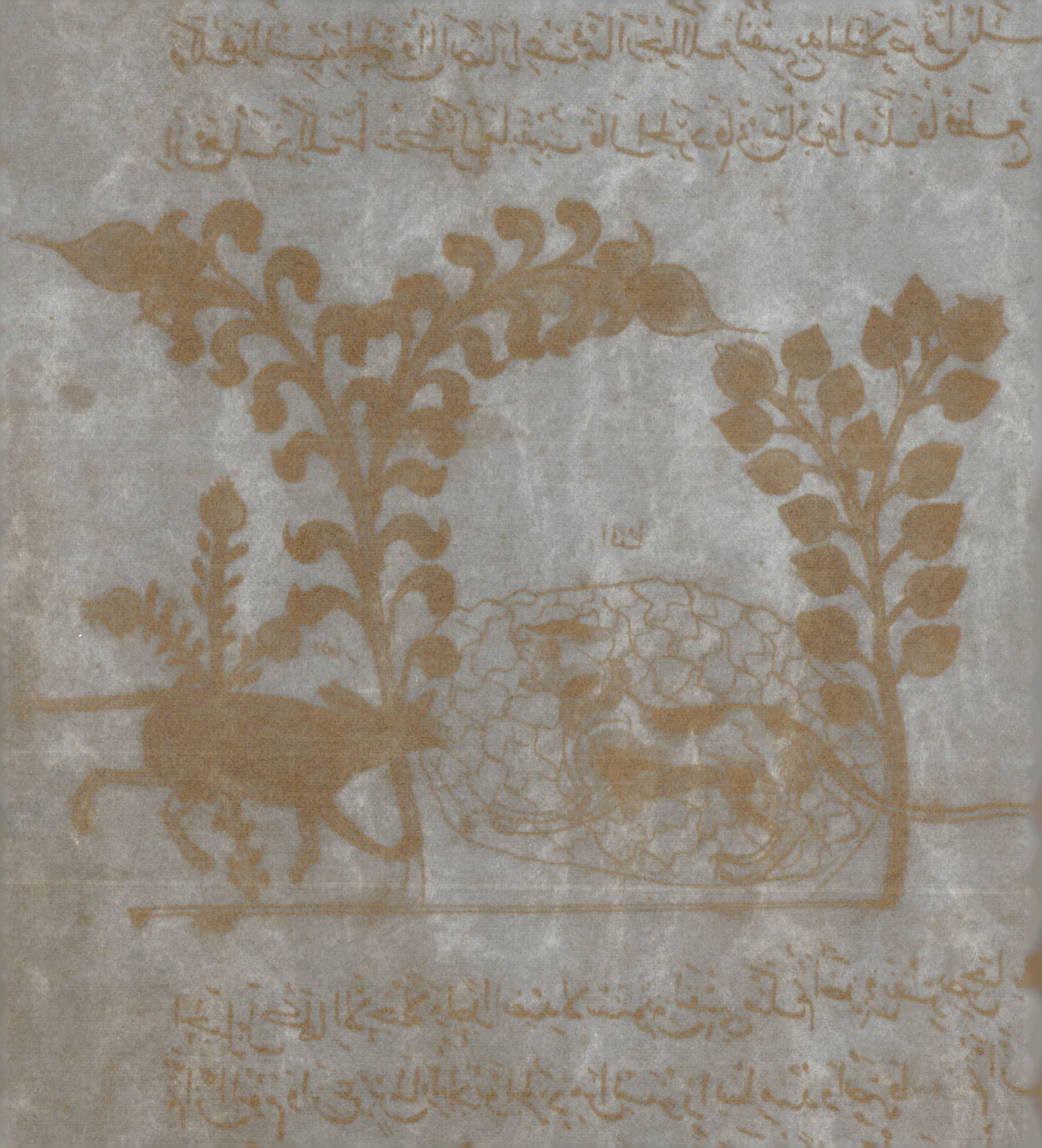

The Prophet Mohammed was a lover of cats. There is a story that one day, when he found a cat asleep on a corner of his robe, he cut the cloth around it rather than wake the cat. That is why, it is said, tabby cats carry the initial M on their foreheads. Mohammed also recommended cats' cohabitation with humans and their acceptance at mosques. And it is said that because of the warm welcome he got from his cats when he returned home, that it is he who granted them the power always to land on their feet.

left *Arabic script from 1350 called* The Cat and the Rat.

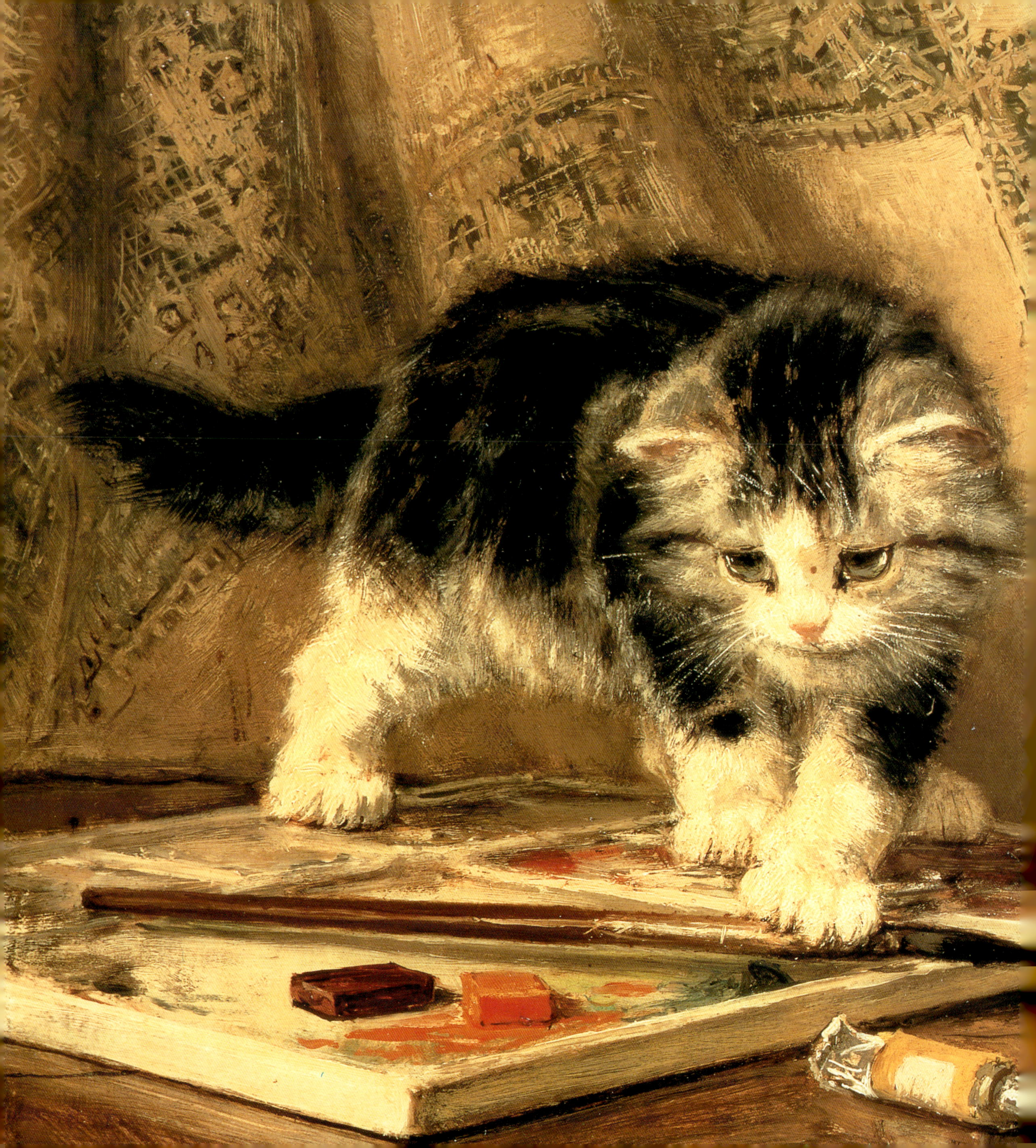

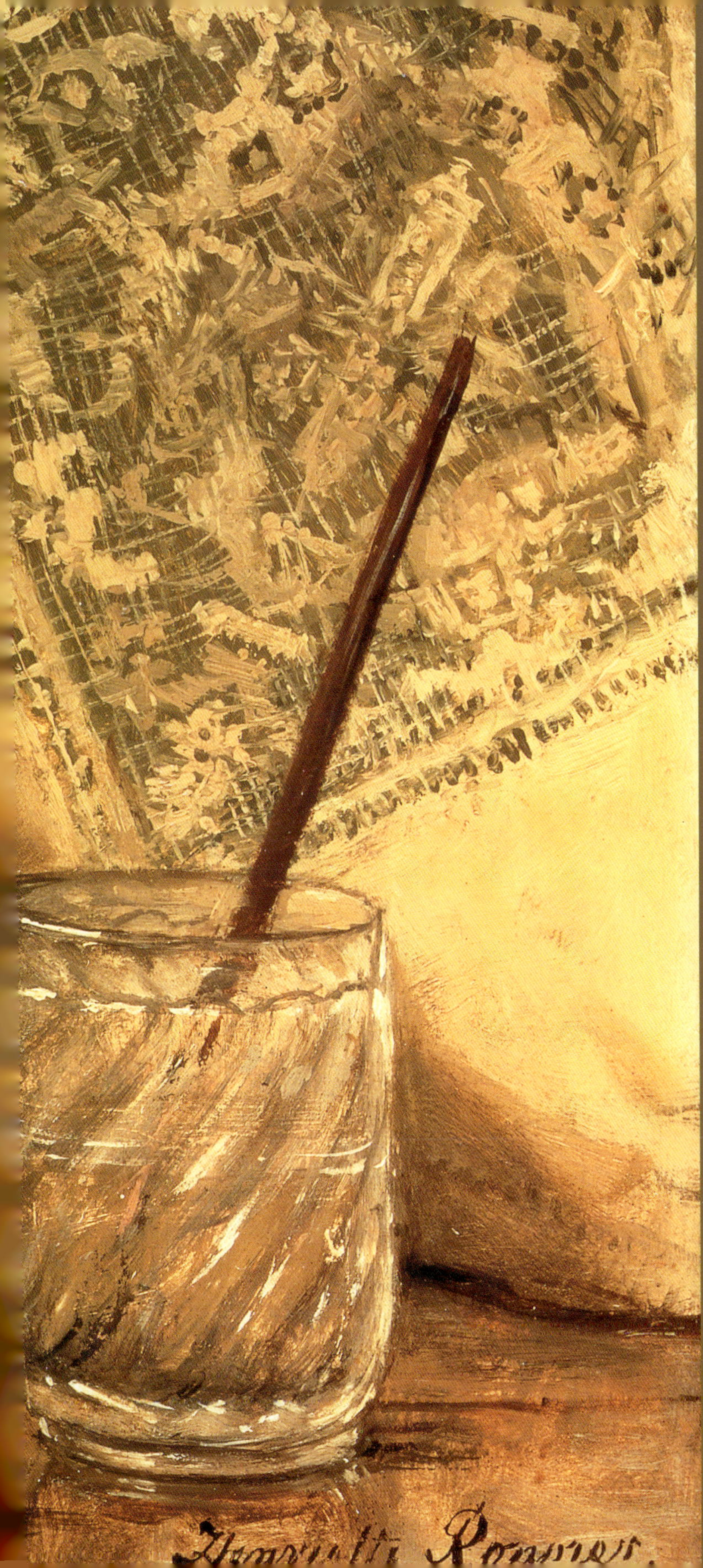

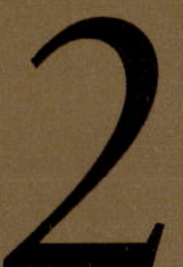
2

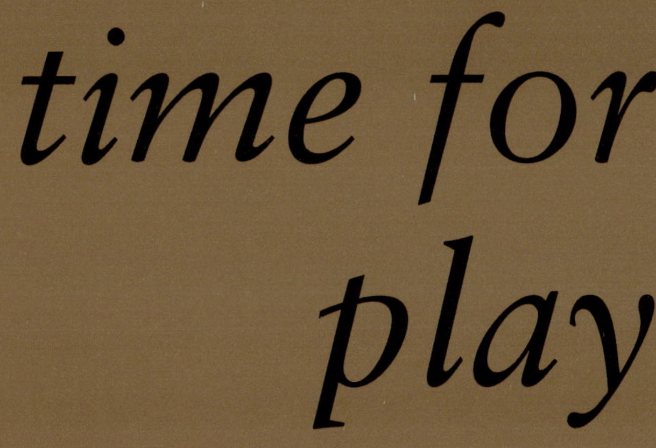
time for
play

previous page *Henriette Ronner-Knip,* The Watercolourist.

right *Another of Ronner-Knip's many cat paintings –* Making Mischief.

That way look, my Infant, lo!
What a pretty baby show!
See the kitten on the wall
Sporting with the leaves that fall,
Withered leaves-one-two-and three –
From the lofty elder tree!...

- But the kitten, how she starts,
Crouches, stretches, paws, and darts!
First at one, and then its fellow
Just a light and just as yellow;
There are many now – now one –
Now they stop and there are none.
What intenseness of desire
In her upward eye of fire!
With a tiger-leap half way
Now she meets the coming prey,
Lets it go as fast, and then
Has it in her power again:
Now she works with three or four,
Like an Indian conjurer,
Quick as he in feats of art,
Far beyond in joy of heart.
Were her antics played in the eye
Of a thousand standers-by,
Clapping hands with shout and stare,
What would little Tabby care
For the plaudits of the crowd?
Over happy to be proud,
Over wealthy in the treasure
Of her own exceeding pleasure!

the kitten and the falling leaves

by William Wordsworth

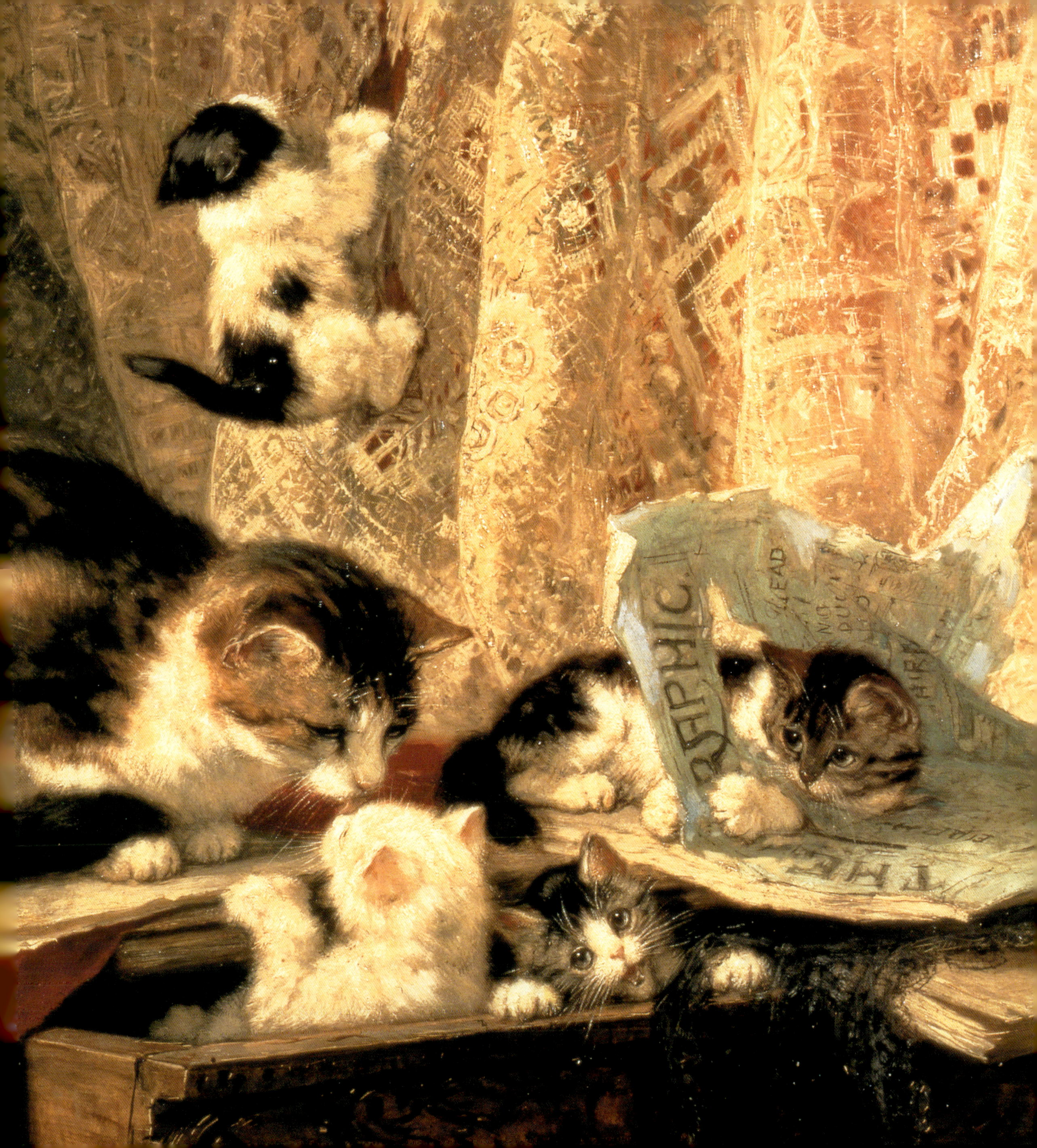
RAPHIC.

right Three Cats, *Franz Marc. The influence of Cezanne is clear in this 1913 painting.*

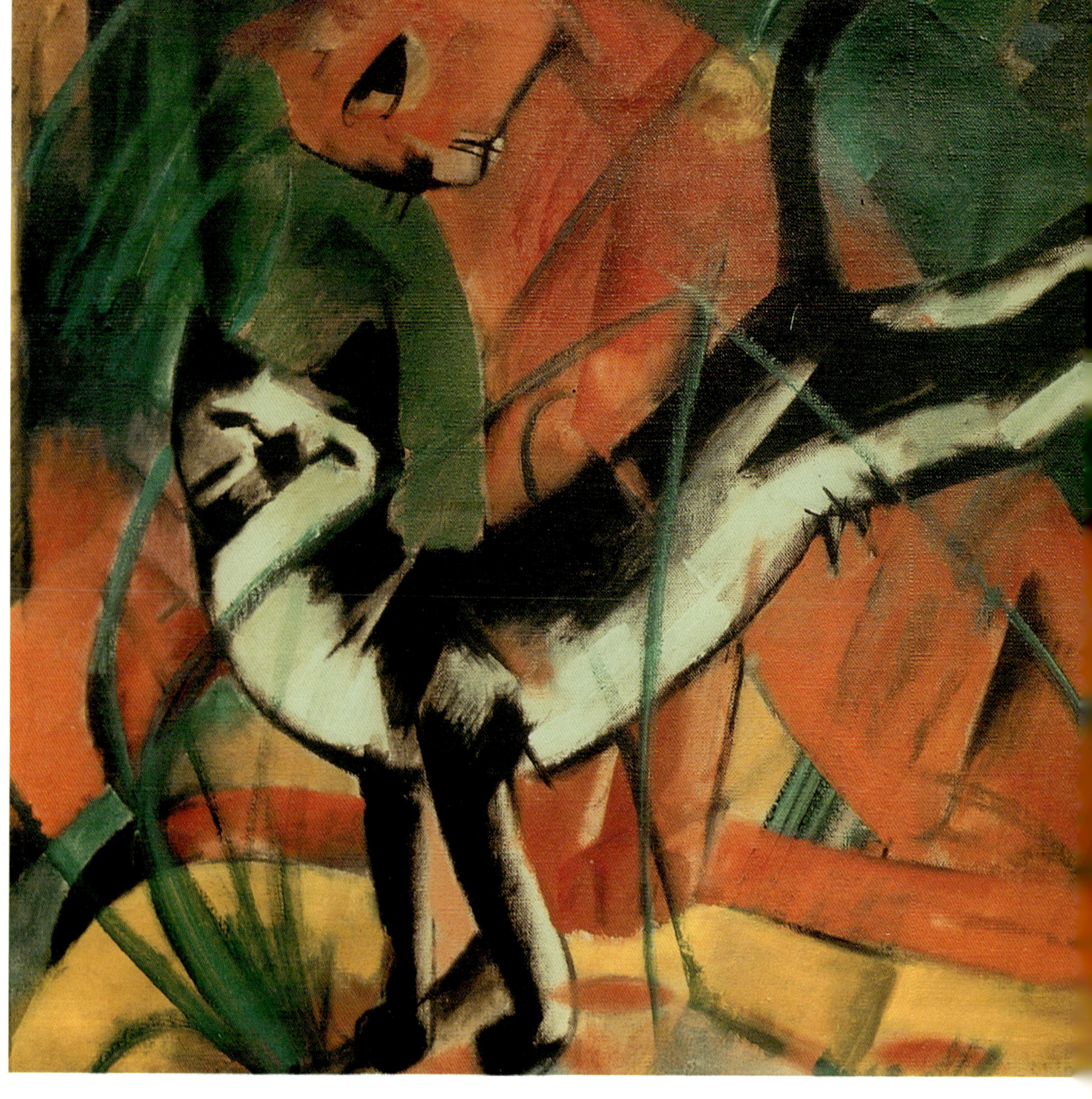

Nearly every one of the colourful canvases painted by Franz Marc (1880-1916) feature animals. Two that depict cats from 1909 and 1910 mark a remarkable transistion in his work. The first shows two cats on a red cloth. The second shows a nude woman giving a saucer of milk to a cat. In 1909, Cezanne's *The Bathers* went on show in Berlin. Marc and the painters of the Bruecke group were strongly influenced by the innocence and purity of Cezannes nudes and sought to emulate them, which Marc does in *Nude with Cat.* Later in 1910, Marc produced his own *Bathing Girls.* By 1912, he was painting a red cat in the arms of a clothed woman, followed by *Two Cats, Blue and Yellow.* By then he had fully developed his unique handling of colour.

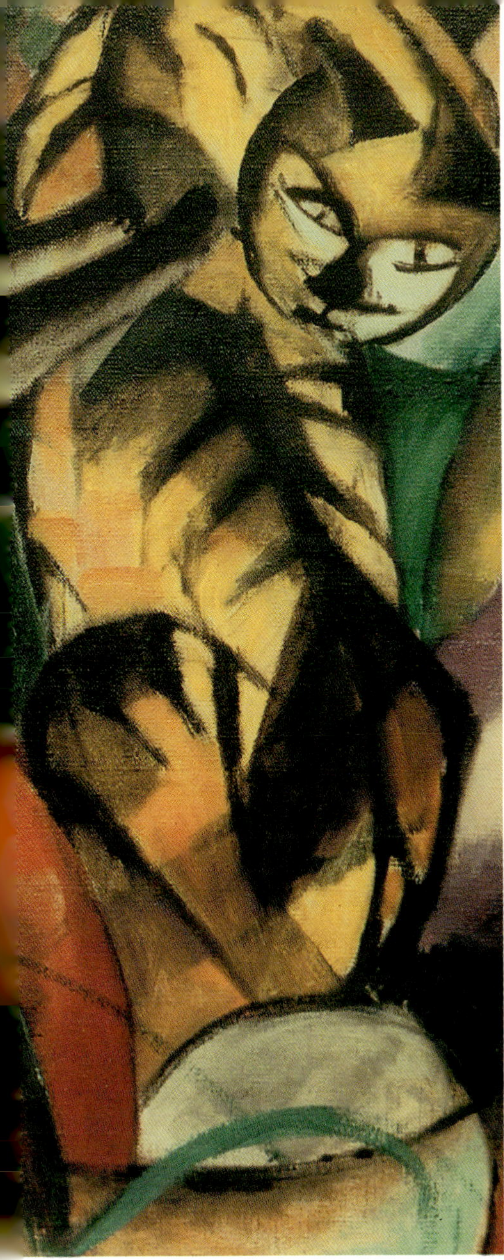

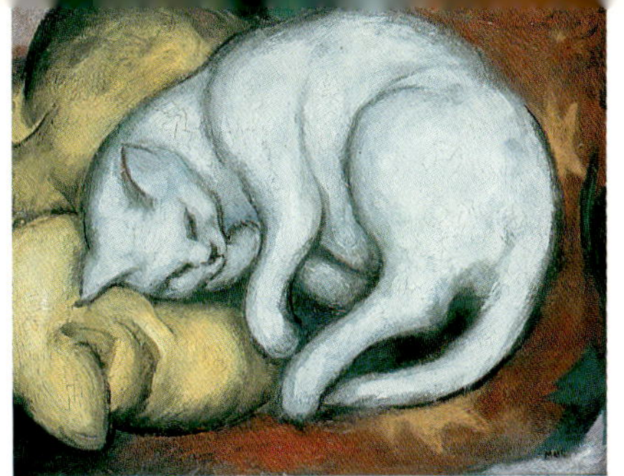

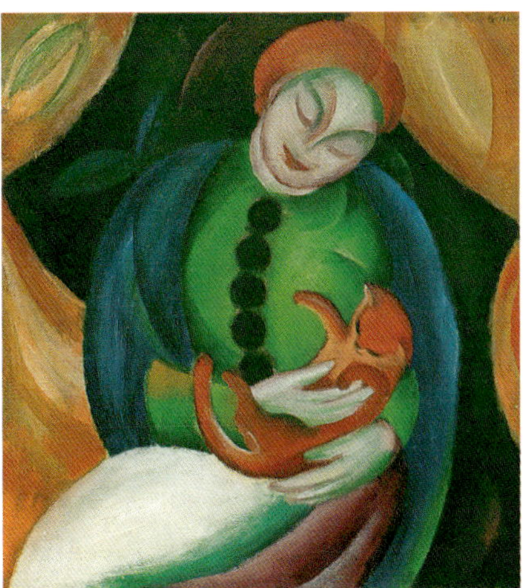

above top Cat on Yellow Pillow, *Marc.*
above Girl with Cat II, *1912, Marc.*

The cat went here and there
And the moon spun round like a top,
And the nearest kin of the moon,
The creeping cat, looked up.
Black Minnaloushe stared at the moon,
For, wander and wail as he would,
The pure cold light in the sky
Troubled his animal blood.
Minnaloushe runs in the grass
Lifting his delicate feet.
Do you dance, Minnaloushe, do you dance?
When the two close kindred meet,
What better than call a dance?
Maybe the moon may learn,
Tired of that courtly fashion,
A new dance turn.
Minnaloushe creeps through the grass
From moolit place to place,
The sacred moon overhead
Has taken a new phase.
Does Minnaloushe know that his pupils
Will pass from change to change,
And that from round to crescent,
From crescent to round they range?
Minnaloushe creeps through the grass
Alone, important and wise,
And lifts to the changing moon
His changing eyes.

the cat and the moon

by W.B. Yeats

right Kitten and Ball of Wool, *Murata Kokodu 1866.*

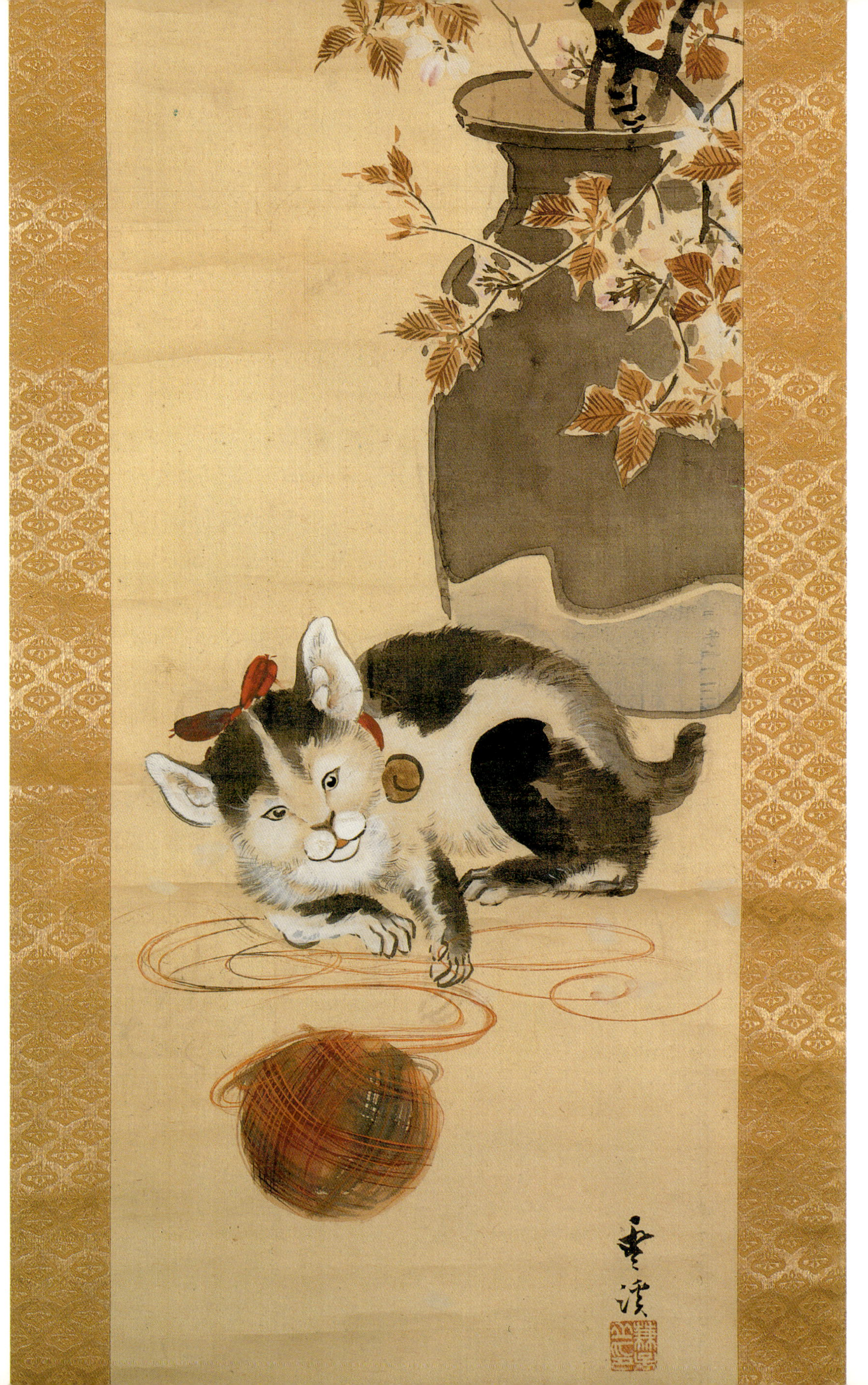

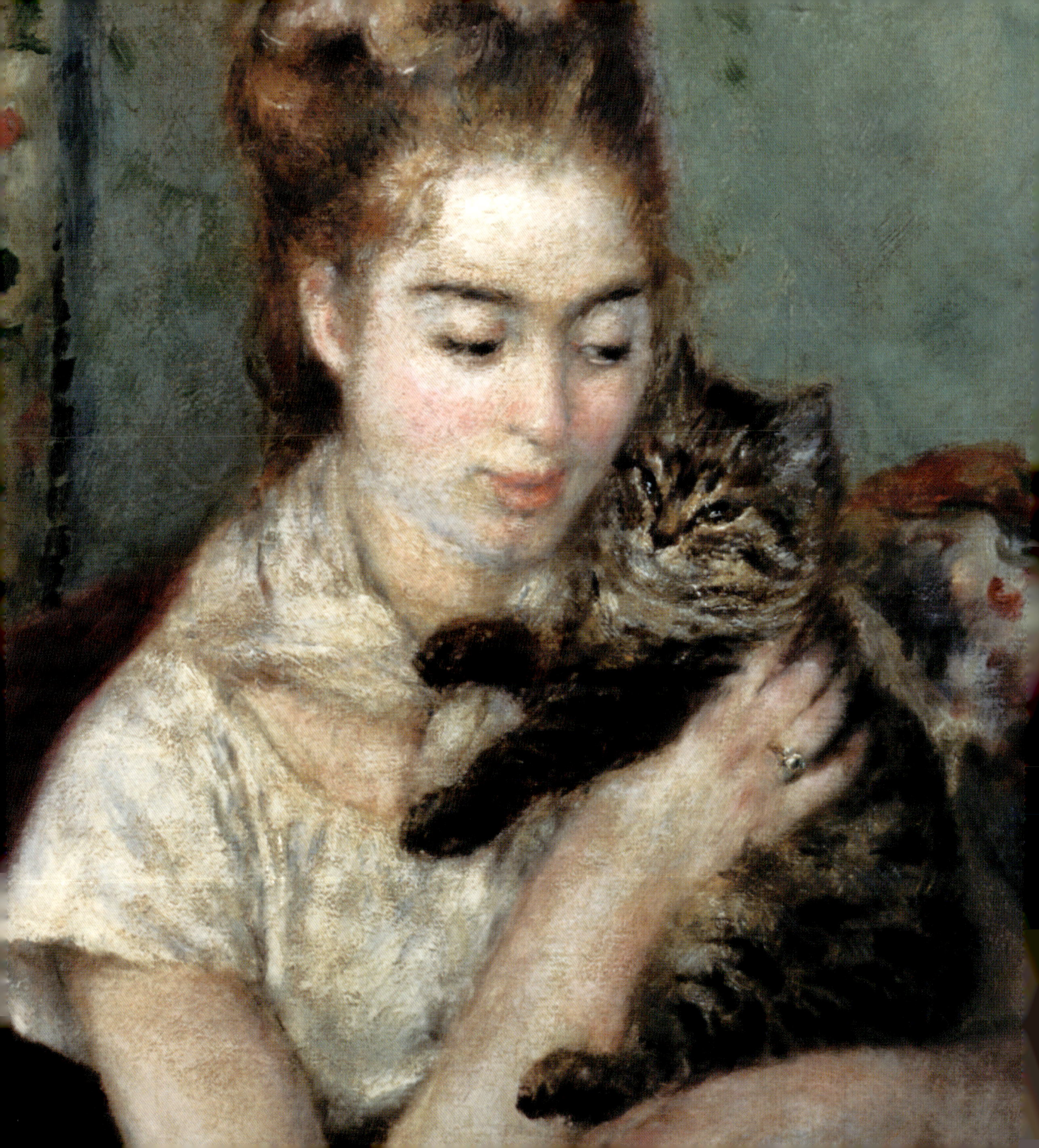

left *Renoir's* Woman with a Cat, *1875.*

In 1882, the French impressionist Pierre Auguste Renoir (1841-1919) completed his *Young Woman with Cat.* In it, he showed his virtuosity in handling paint. The auburn-haired young woman's fair skin is treated so sensuously that it has the texture of the skin of a peach. But the sharp focus of the painting is the head of the tortoiseshell cat she is watching as it scales a flower pot. At some points, the paint is so thin that the canvas is allowed to show through. On the cat's back though, the paint is built up in the thick impasto. The young woman is Renoir's mistress Aline Charigot, who he married in 1890. The name of the tortoiseshell cat that seems to fascinate her so is not recorded.

below Young Woman with Cat, *1882, Renoir.*

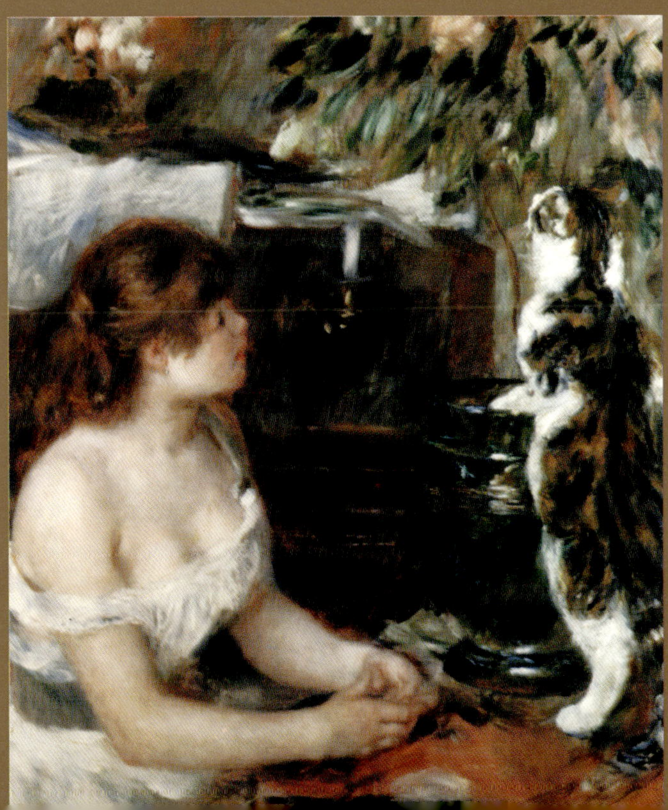

3

explorers

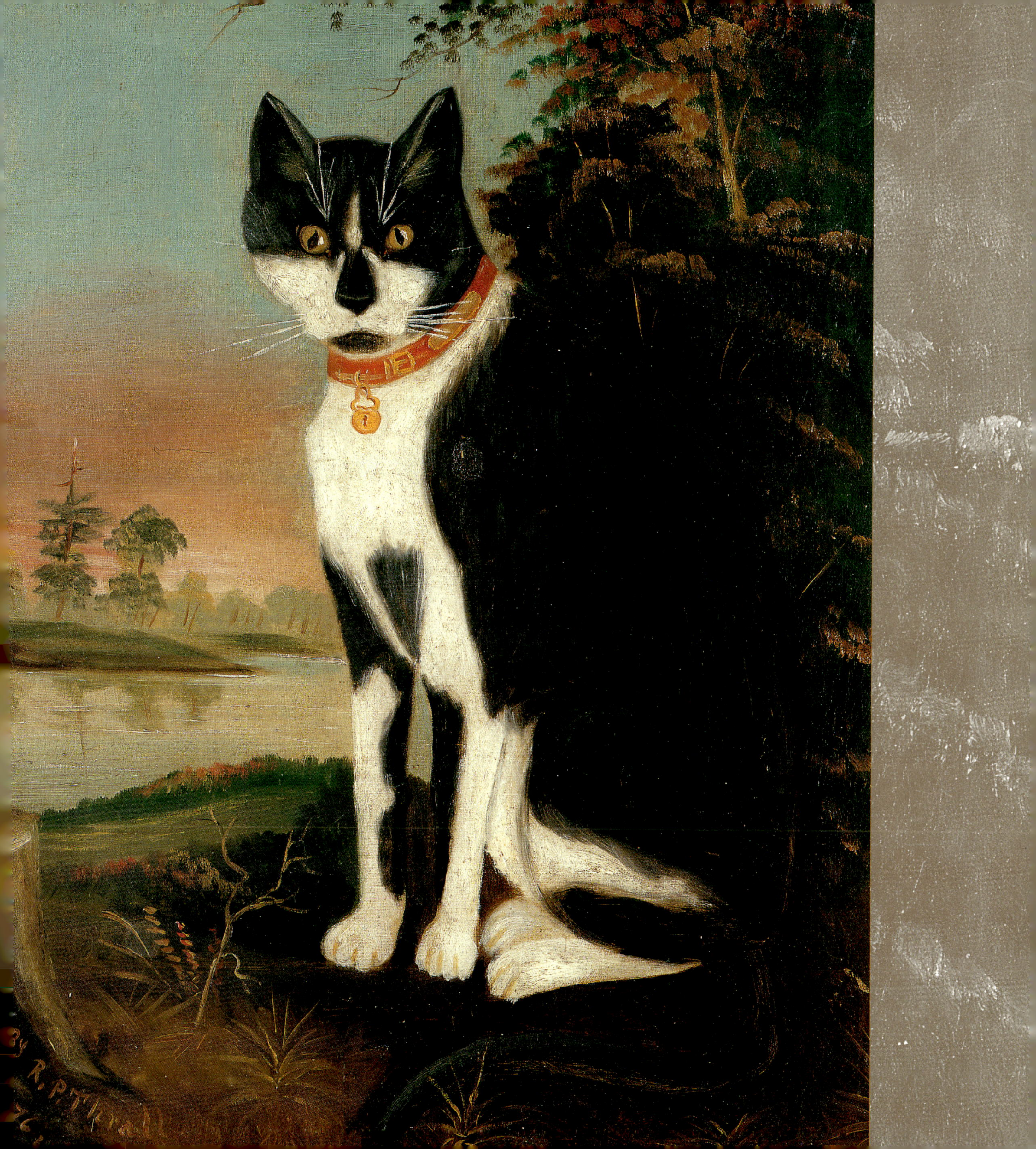

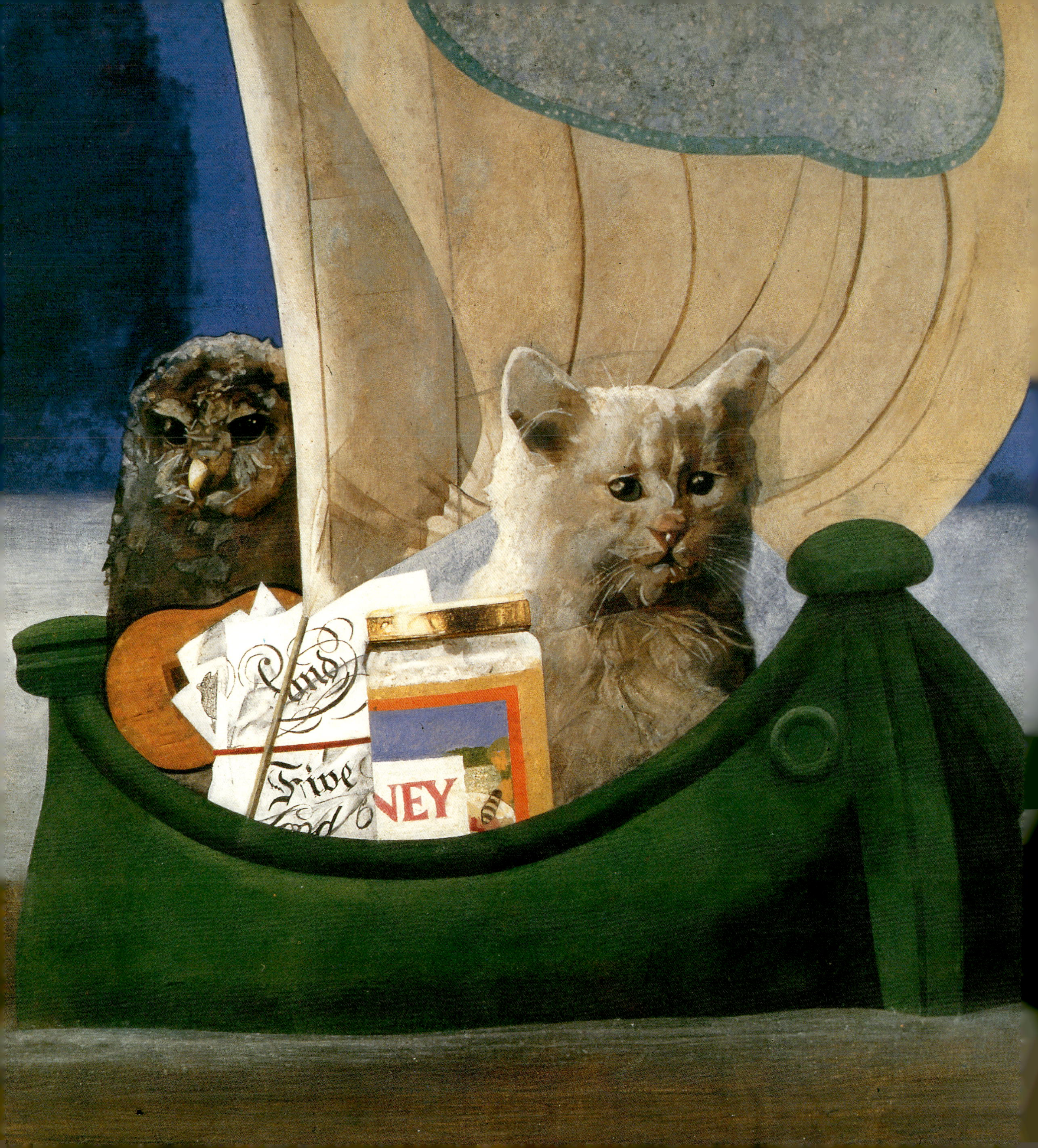

and
Five
NEY

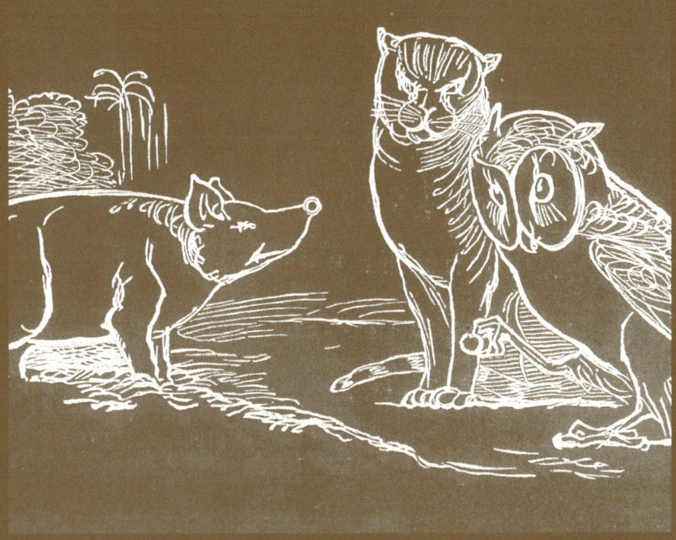

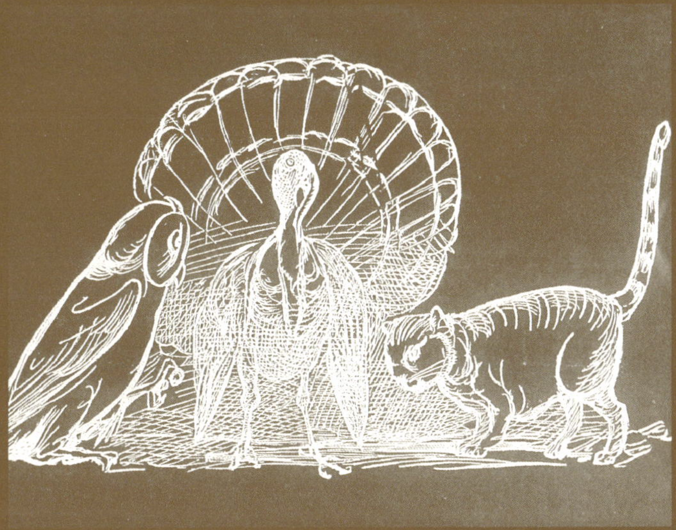

previous page Minnie from the Outskirts of the Village, *painting of a cat by RP Thrall – USA.*

above *Edward Lear's own illustrations of* The Owl and the Pussycat *from his* Nonsense Songs and Stories.

left The Owl and the Pussycat *by Peter Blake – 20th Century.*

The Owl and the Pussycat
The Owl and the Pussycat went to sea
In a beautiful pea-green boat:
They took some honey and plenty of money
Wrapped up in a five-pound note.
The Owl looked up to the stars above,
And sang to a small guitar,
'Oh lovely Pussy, O Pussy, my love,
What a beautiful Pussy you are,
You are,
You are!
What a beautiful Pussy you are!'

Pussy said to the Owl, 'You elegant fowl,
How charmingly sweet you sing!
Oh! let us be married; too long we have tarried:
But what shall we do for a ring?'
They sailed away for a year and a day,
To the land where the bong-tree grows;
And there in a wood a Piggy-wig stood,
With a ring at the end of his nose,
His nose,
His nose,
With a ring at the end of his nose.

'Dear Pig, are you willing to sell for one shilling
'Your ring?' Said the Piggy, 'I will.'
So they took it away, and were married next day
By the Turkey who lives on the hill.
They dined on mince and slices of quince,
Which they ate with a runcible spoon;
And hand in hand, on the edge of the sand,
They danced by the light of the moon,
The moon,
The moon,
They danced by the light of the moon.

the owl and the pussycat

Edward Lear

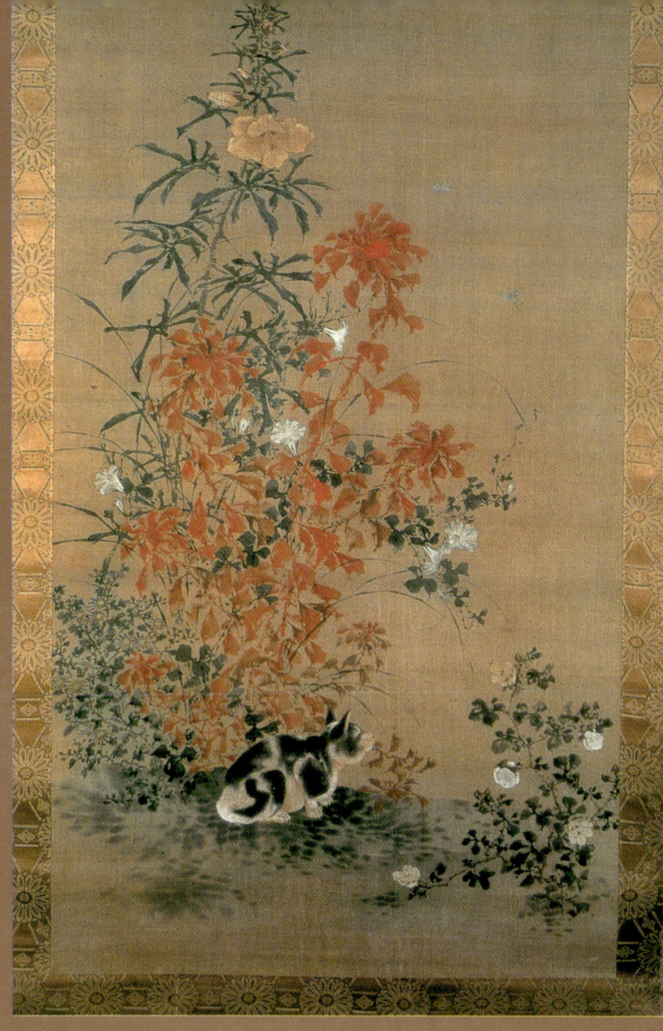

above Cat Amidst Flowers, *Rantokuza.*

Cats appear frequently in early Japanese prints. They are usually the playthings of the courtesans who are the traditional subject matter of Japanese printmaking. But in his ground-breaking series Famous Sites of Edo: One Hundred Views, the famous Japanese printmaker Ando Hiroshige (1797-1858) shows a fat white cat on its own, looking out of a courtesan's window in the city of Edo, now called Tokyo. Below him, there are thousands of holiday makers returning from the Tori no Machi festival. Beyond, across a vast landscape, gleams Mount Fuji. Using such simple devices, Hiroshige took printmaking out of the quarter, where it had belonged up until then, and out into the natural world. Hiroshige turned his back on the kabuki players and the geisha of the red light district and turned his attention to landscape. He then travelled widely around Japan and met the wild life painters of Kyoto. Under their influence, he produced prints of animals and flowers. After Hiroshige cats are often depicted on their own in Japanese art, without their courtesan owners.

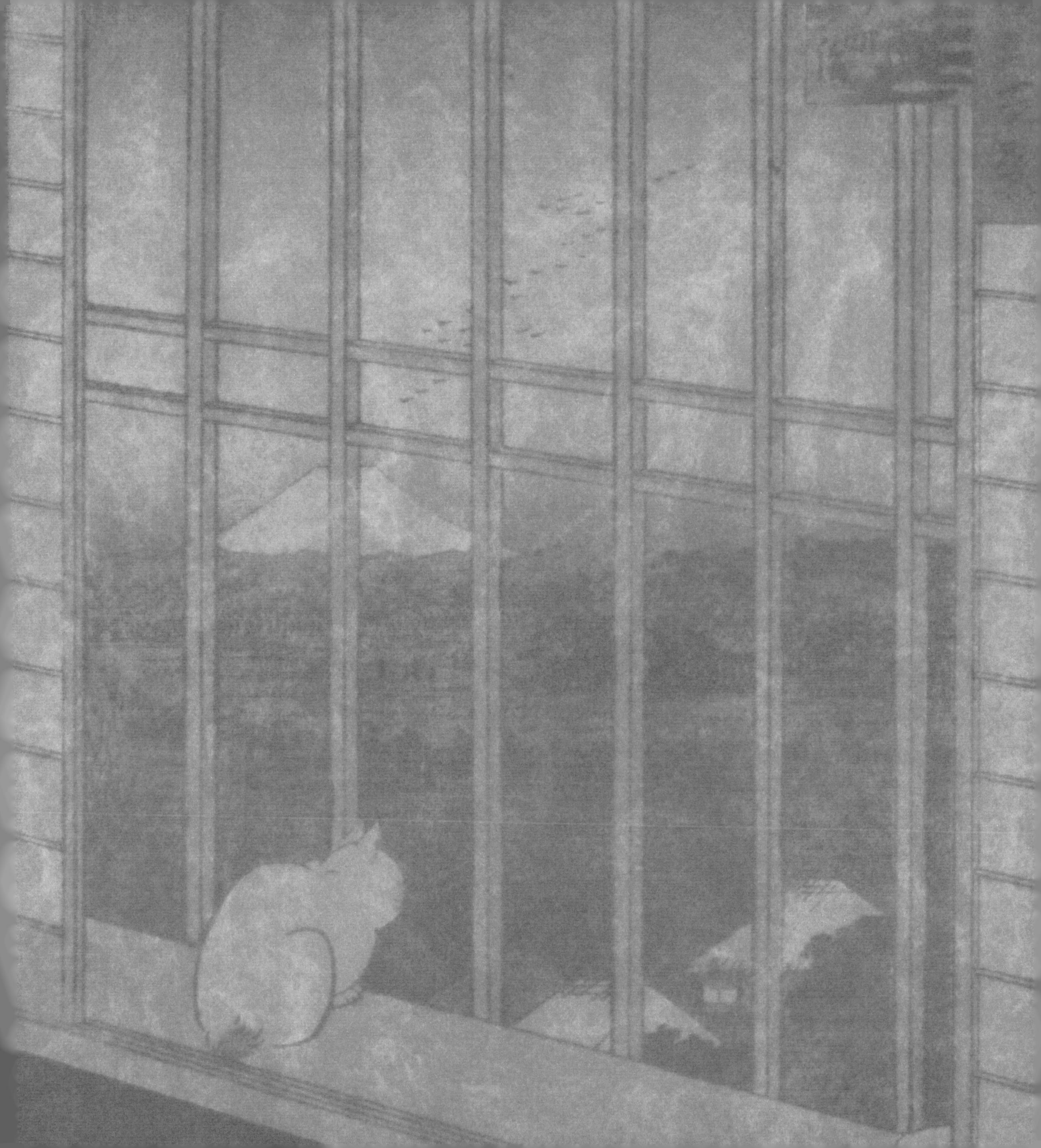

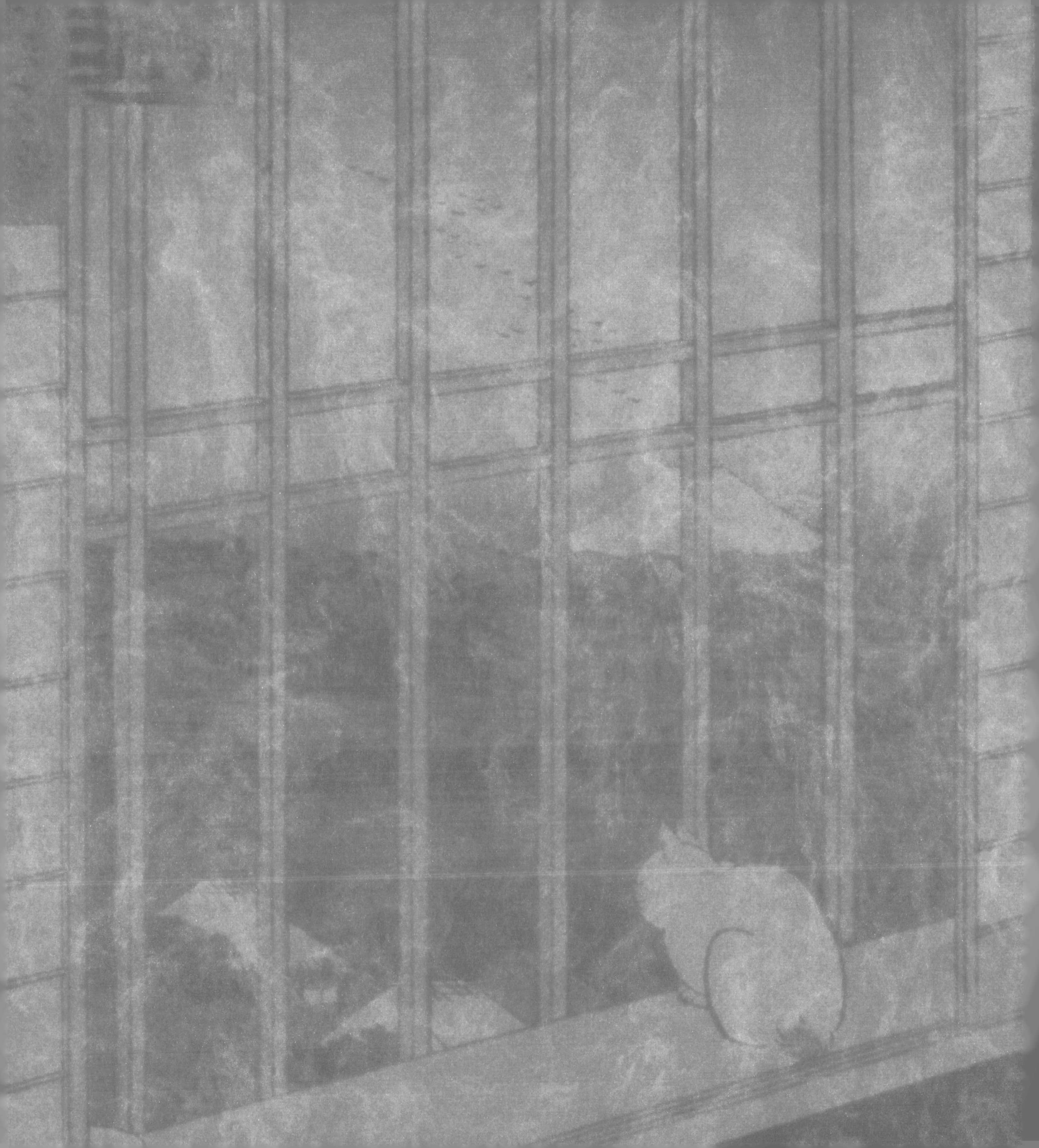

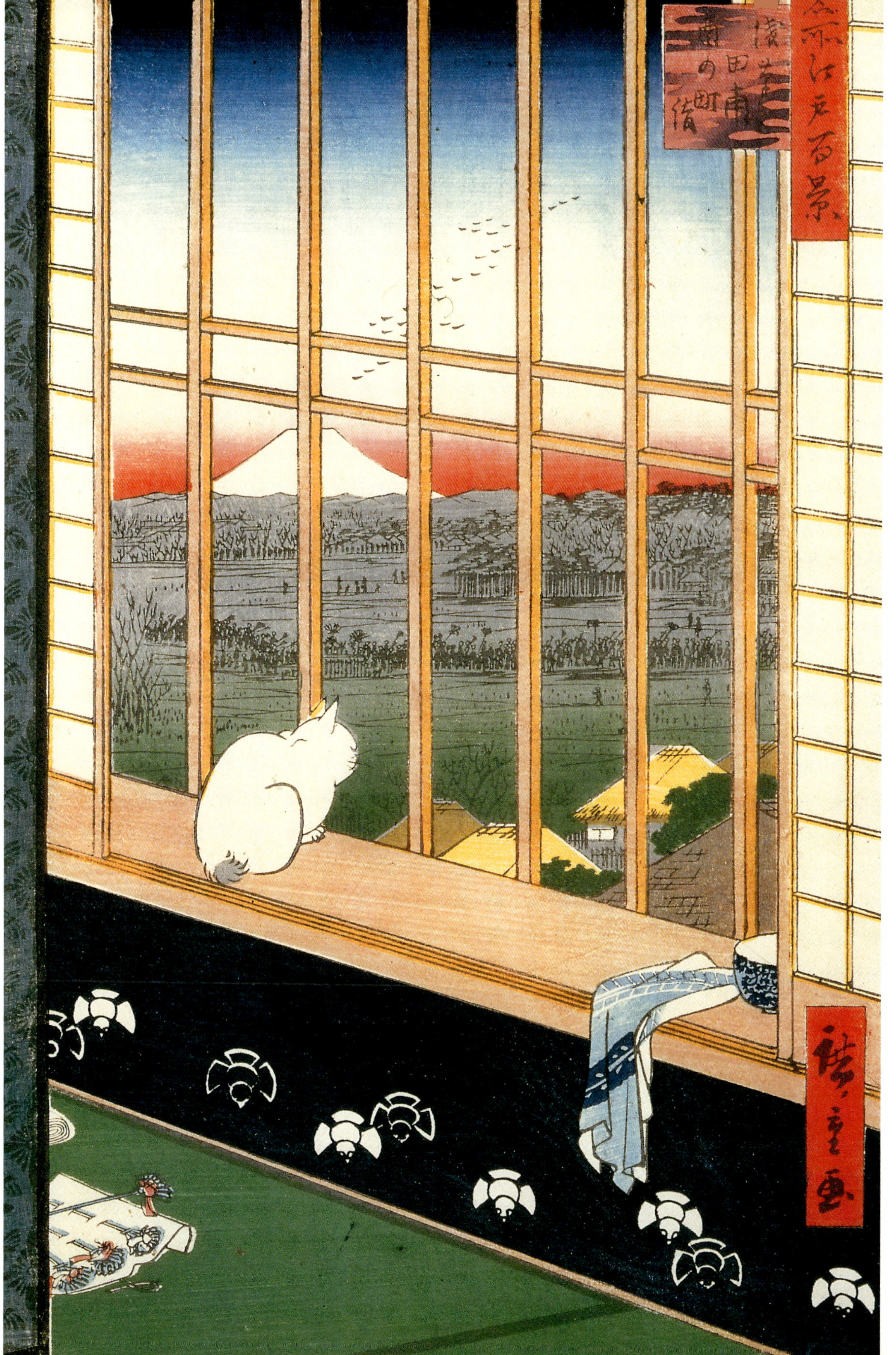

left *A Japanese print by Hiroshige* – Cat on a windowsill *from the series* 100 Views of Edo, *published 1857.*

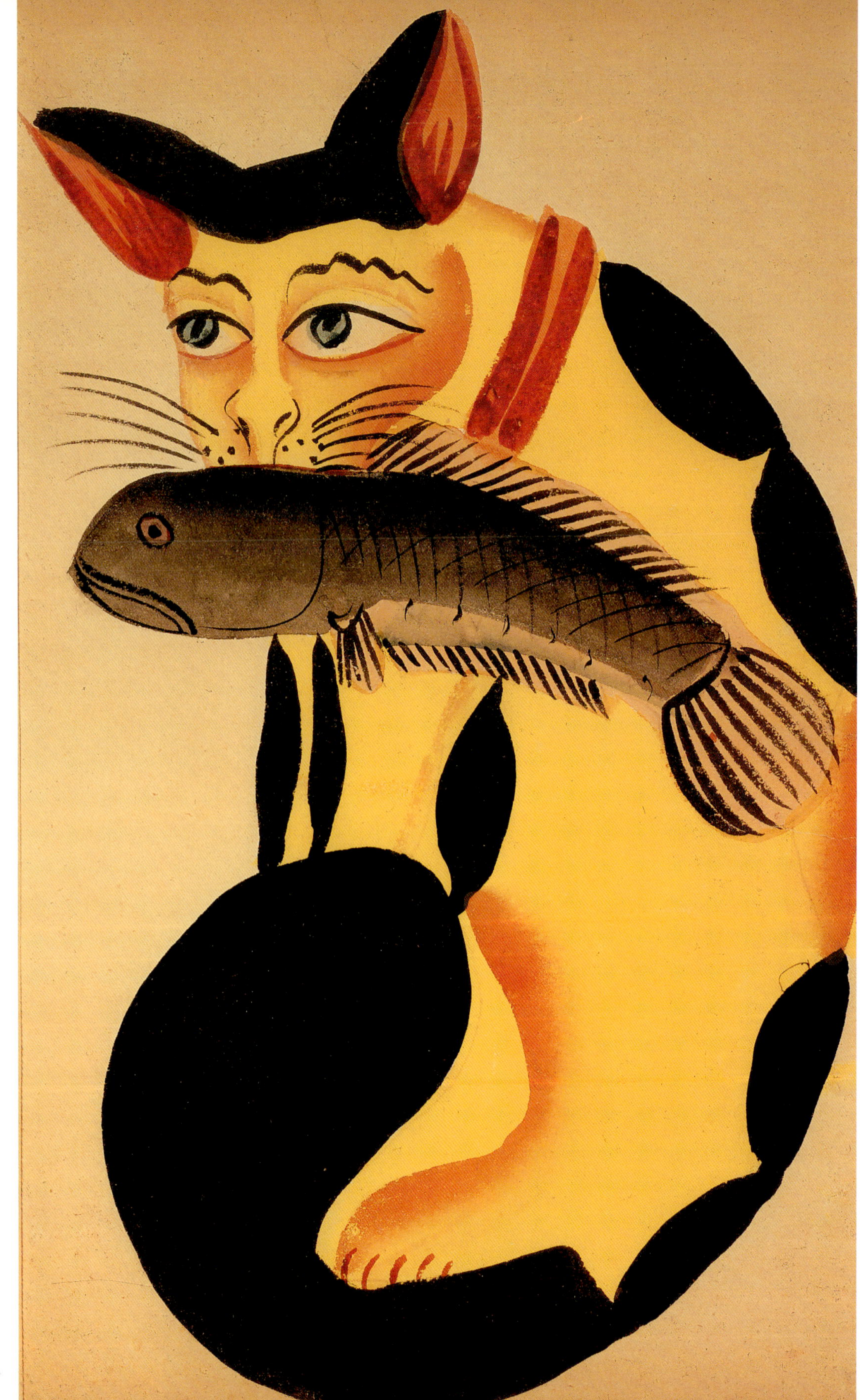

In *The Cat That Walked by Himself*, Rudyard Kipling tells of how Woman tamed the Man and the Dog, but the Cat insisted on retaining its independence. However, he promised to be kind to babies (as long as they do not pull his tail too hard) if he was allowed to sit by the fire and drink warm milk three times day.

The Cat... said, 'I will catch mice when I am in the Cave for always and always and always; but still I am the Cat who walks by himself, and all places are alike to me.'

'Not when I am near,' said the Man. 'If you had not said that last I would have put all these things away for always and always and always; but I am now going to throw my two boots and my little stone axe (that makes three) at you whenever I meet you. And so shall all proper Men do after me!'

Then the Dog said, 'Wait a minute. He has not make a bargain with me or with all proper Dogs after me.' And he showed his teeth and said, 'If you are not kind to the Baby while I am in the Cave for always and always and always, I will hunt you till I catch you, and when I catch you I will bite you. And so shall all proper Dogs do after me.'

'Ah,' said the Woman, listening, 'this is a very clever Cat, but he is not so clever as the Dog.'

Cat counted the Dog's teeth (and they looked very pointed) and he said, 'I will be kind to the Baby while I am in the Cave, as long as he does not pull my tail too hard, for always and always and always. But still I am the Cat that walks by himself, and all places are alike to me.'

'Not when I am near,' said the Dog. 'If you had not said that last I would have shut my mouth for always and always and always; but now I am going to hunt you up a tree whenever I meet you. And so shall all proper Dogs do after me.'

Then the Man threw his two boots and his little stone axe (that makes three) at the Cat, and the Cat ran out of the Cave, and the Dog chased him up a tree; and from that day to this, Best Beloved, three proper Men out of five will always throw things at a Cat whenever they meet him, and all proper Dogs will chase him up a tree. But the Cat keeps his side of the bargain too. He will kill mice, and he will be kind to Babies when he is in the house, just so long as they do not pull his tail too hard. But when he has done that, and between times, and when the moon gets up and night comes, he is the Cat that walks by himself, and all places are alike to him. Then he goes out to the Wet Wild Woods or up on the Wet Wild Trees or on the Wet Wild Roofs, waving his wild tail and walking by his wild lone.

left A Cat with a Fish in its Mouth, *from the Rudyard Kipling collection, Calcutta c. 1890.*

right *A tile panel of a cat from Palacio Frontiera Lisbon – 18th Century.*

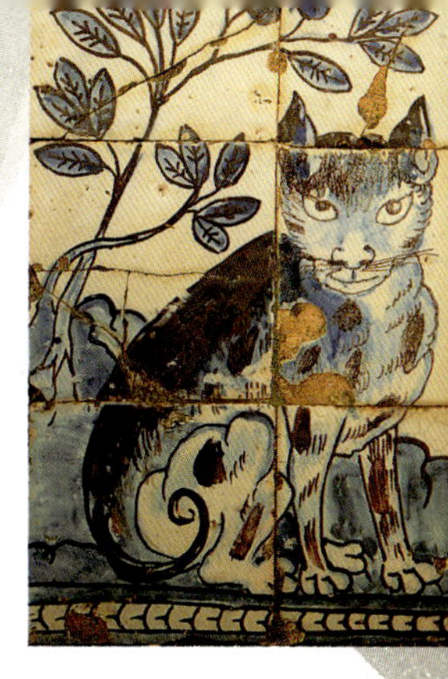

'a cat in gloves catches no mice.'

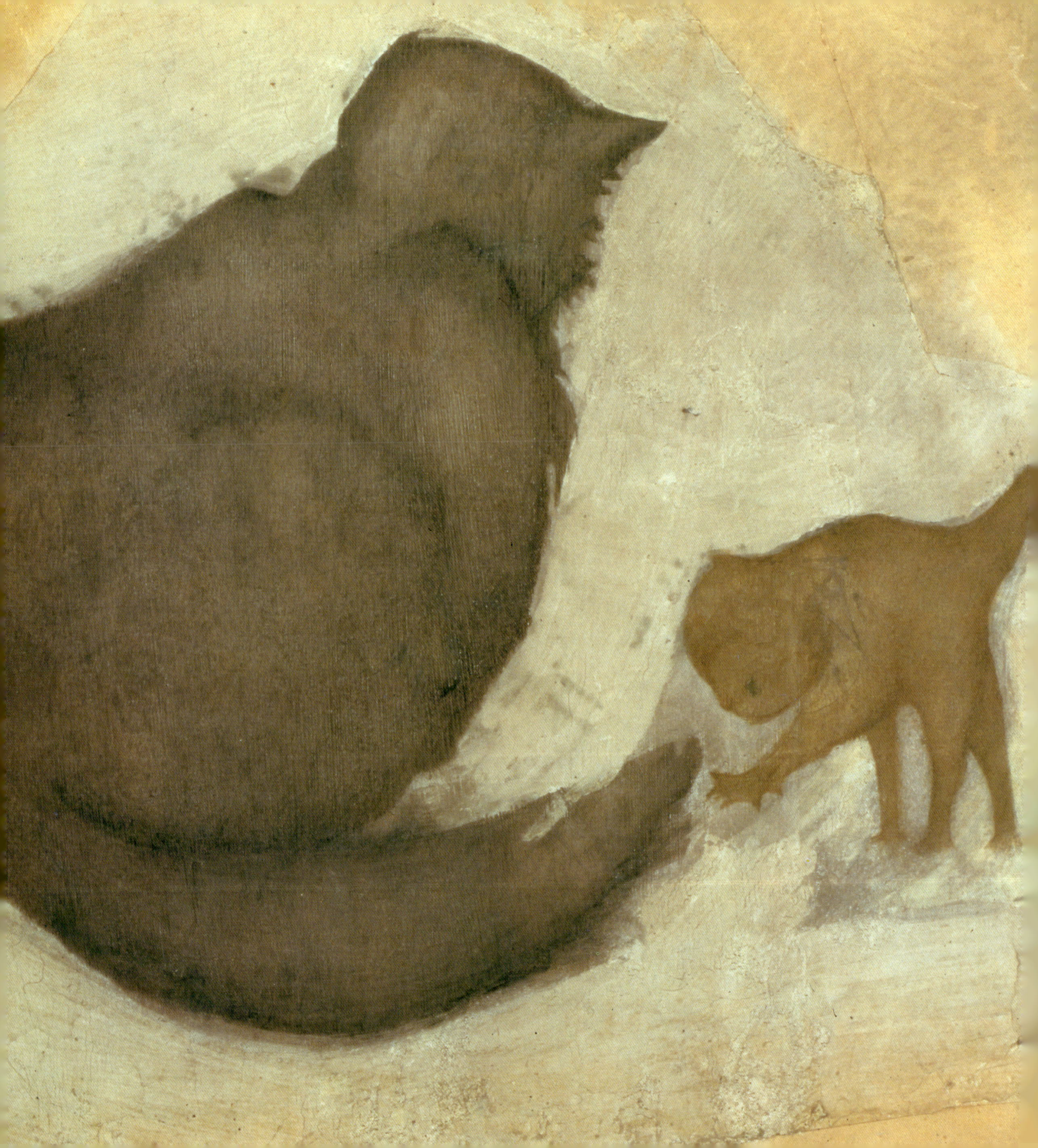

Even the laziest cat can be tempted from its sloth by the sight of a scurrying mouse, fluttering bird or some other delicacy. In a second, centuries of domestication fall away and the old, wild instincts come to the fore, transforming the cat from the very image of indolence into a cunning, lean, mean hunter.

Stealth and athletic ability are the cat's allies here, and it also has a formidable armoury of weapons at its disposal. To maximize its speed, it literally runs on its toes, leaving other, slower carnivores to lumber along behind. It's flexible leg joints allow it to climb and spring, even from a standing start, while within each fluffy toe is concealed a precision tool: a razor-sharp claw designed to seize and grip, and with the clever added design feature of being retractable when not in use. Two canine teeth make short work of the job of killing, while four cheek teeth called carnassials work like scissor blades, sliding past each other to slice the flesh.

Such prowess has made the cat a useful beast to have around on the farm or in the kitchen, to keep the rodent population down. Its hunting skills have even, in some cases, elevated it to legendary status. In the famous story of Puss-in-Boots, Puss engineers his master's rise to the landowning aristocracy by tricking a rich – but gullible – ogre into changing into a mouse. The cat belonging to Dick Whittington, a character based on a real person, transformed his master from pauper to Lord Mayor of London by dispensing with an entire island-full of rats.

A statue to this famous feline hunter still stands on Highgate Hill in London.

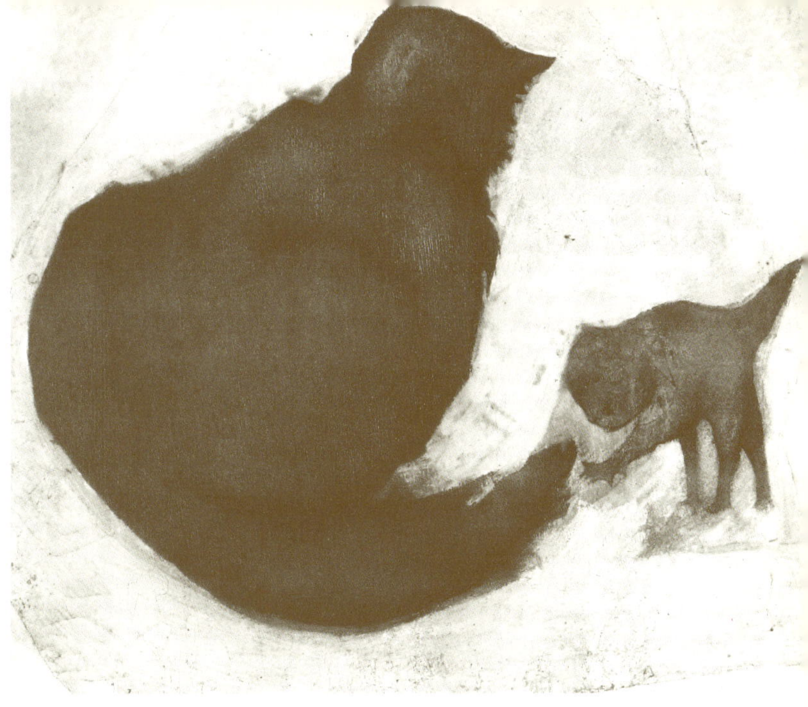

above *A 19th Century watercolour by Sir Edward Burne-Jones* – Cat and Kitten.

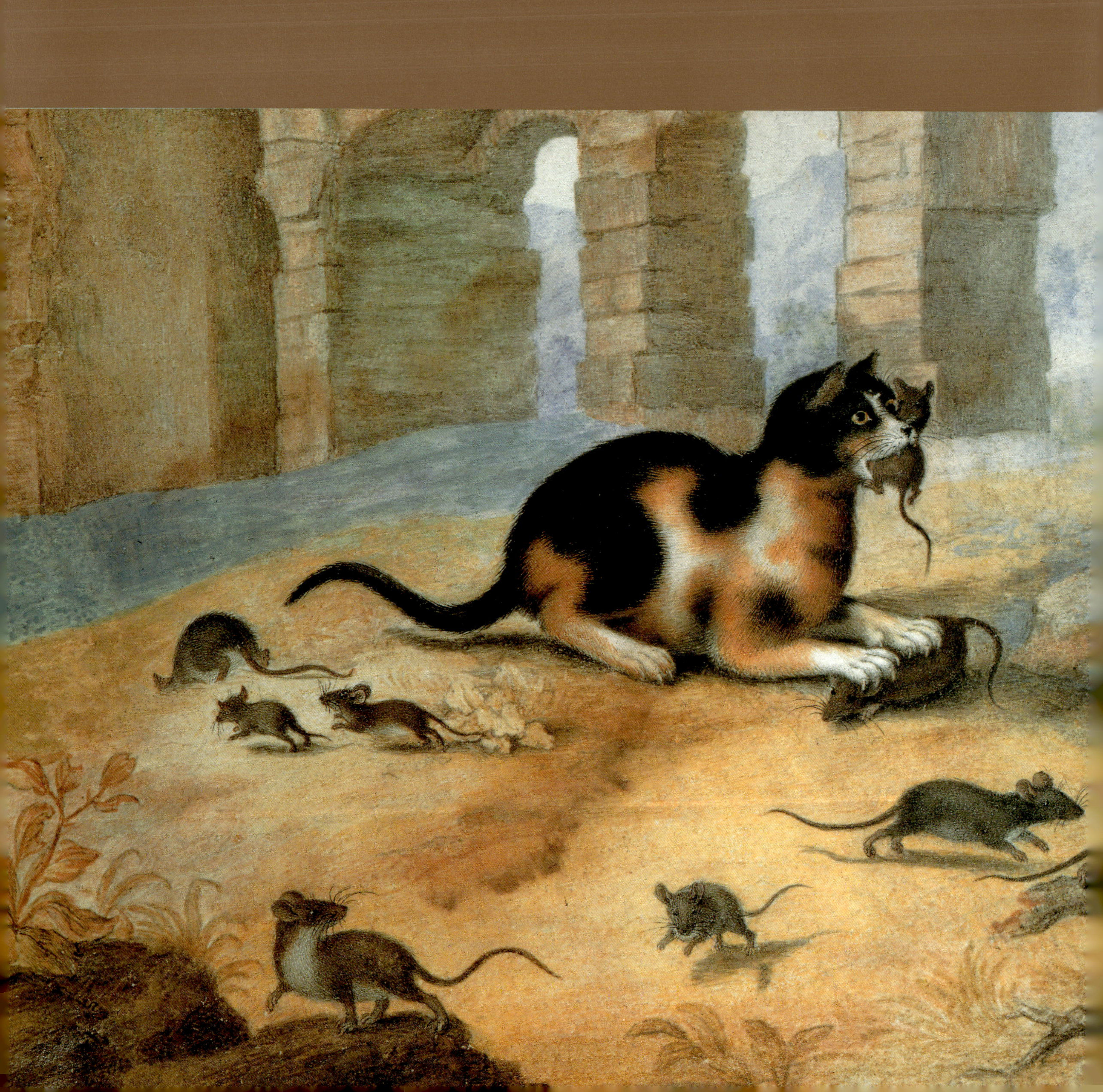

prowlers

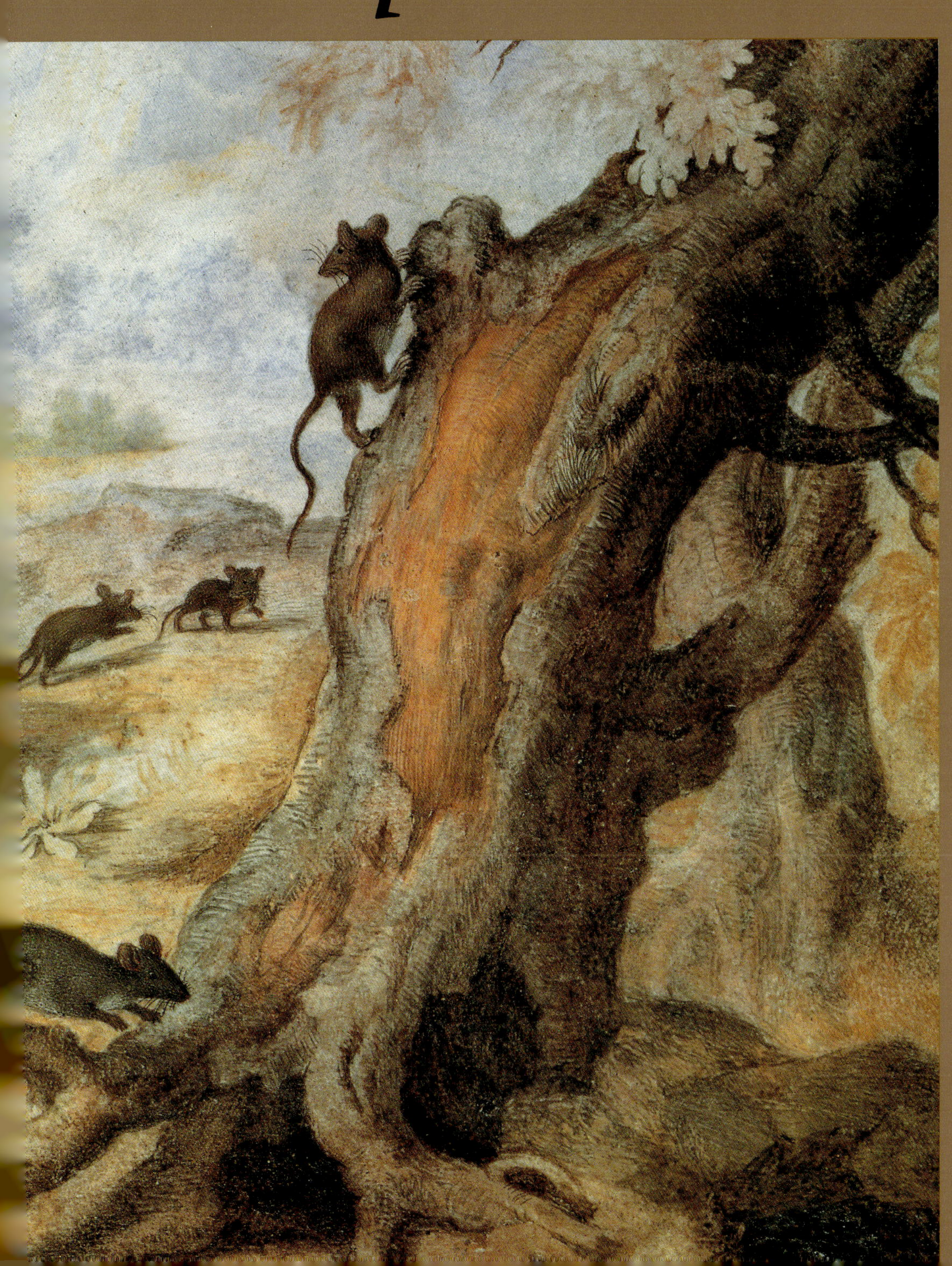

4

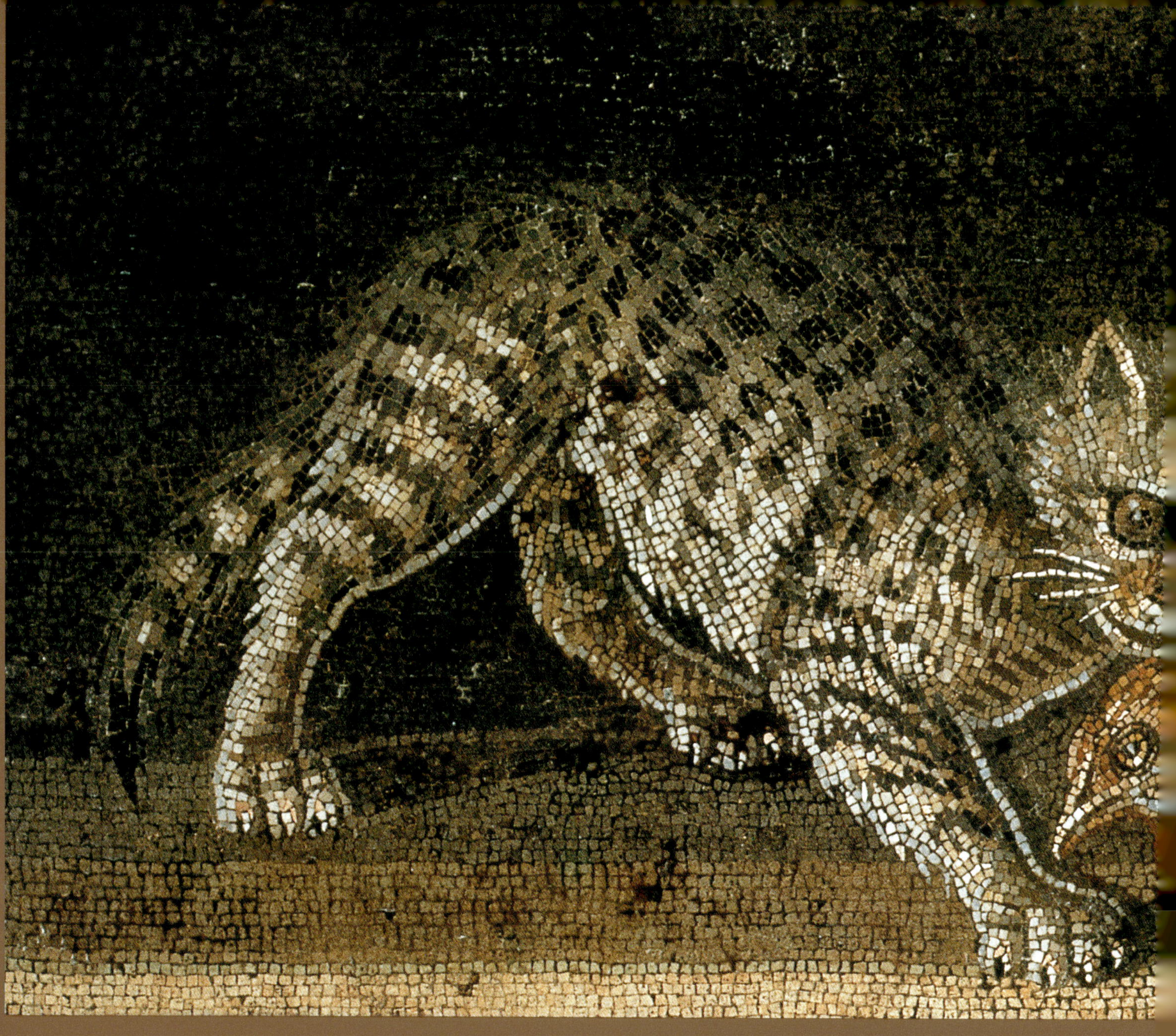

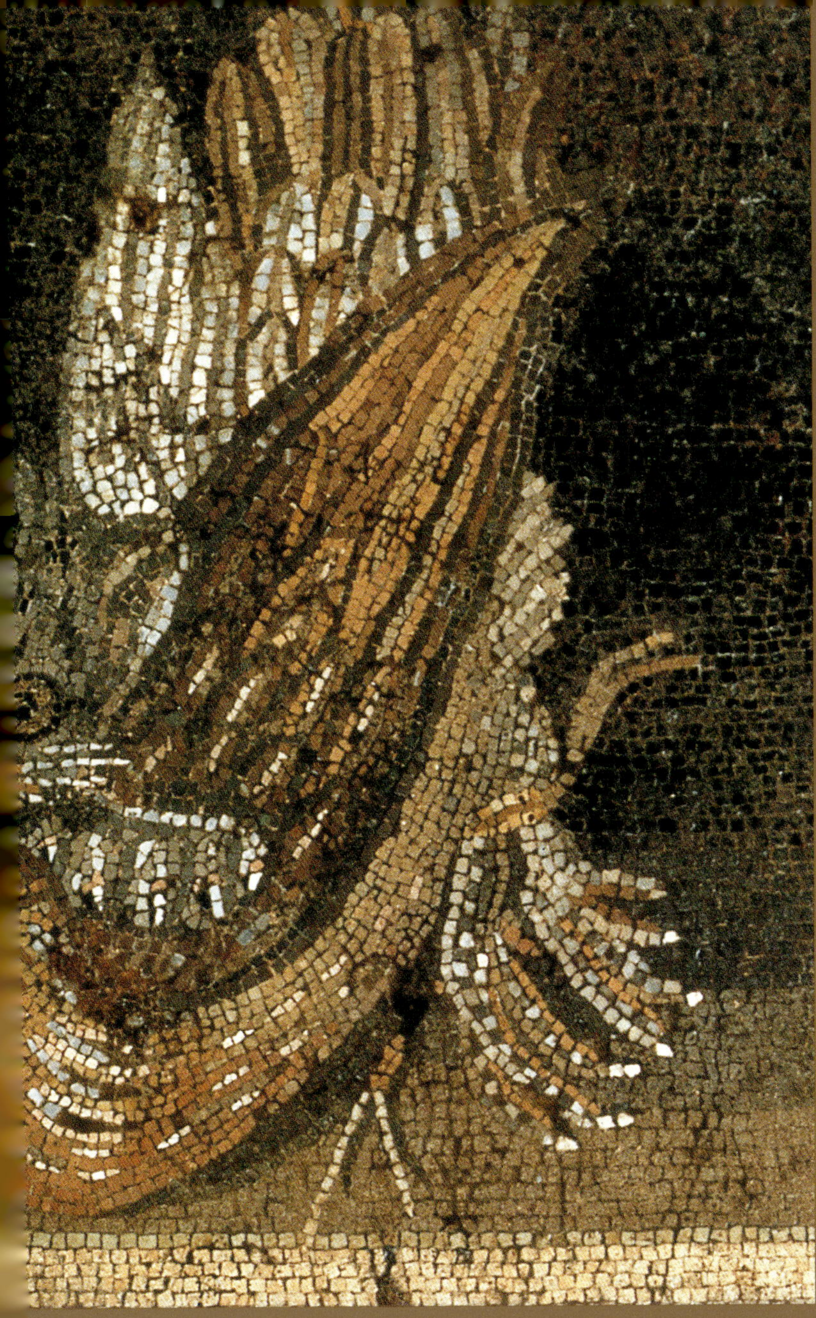

previous page Cat killing Mice in a Landscape, *by Swiss artist Gottfried Mindt.*

left *Detail of a Roman mosaic from Pompeii – from the 1st Century.*

The Roman naturalist Pliny makes no mention of cats, other than one reference to the golden cat – possibly a wild cat – revered by the Arabs. A mosaic of a tabby cat was found in Pompeii. But, strangely, no remains of cats have been found in the ruins there and what part they played in Roman life is unknown. However, it is known that the Roman legions introduced cats to Northern Europe and it is said that there were no cats in Britain before the invasion of Julius Caesar. However, the remains of a cat were found in a Roman villa at Lullingworth in Kent.

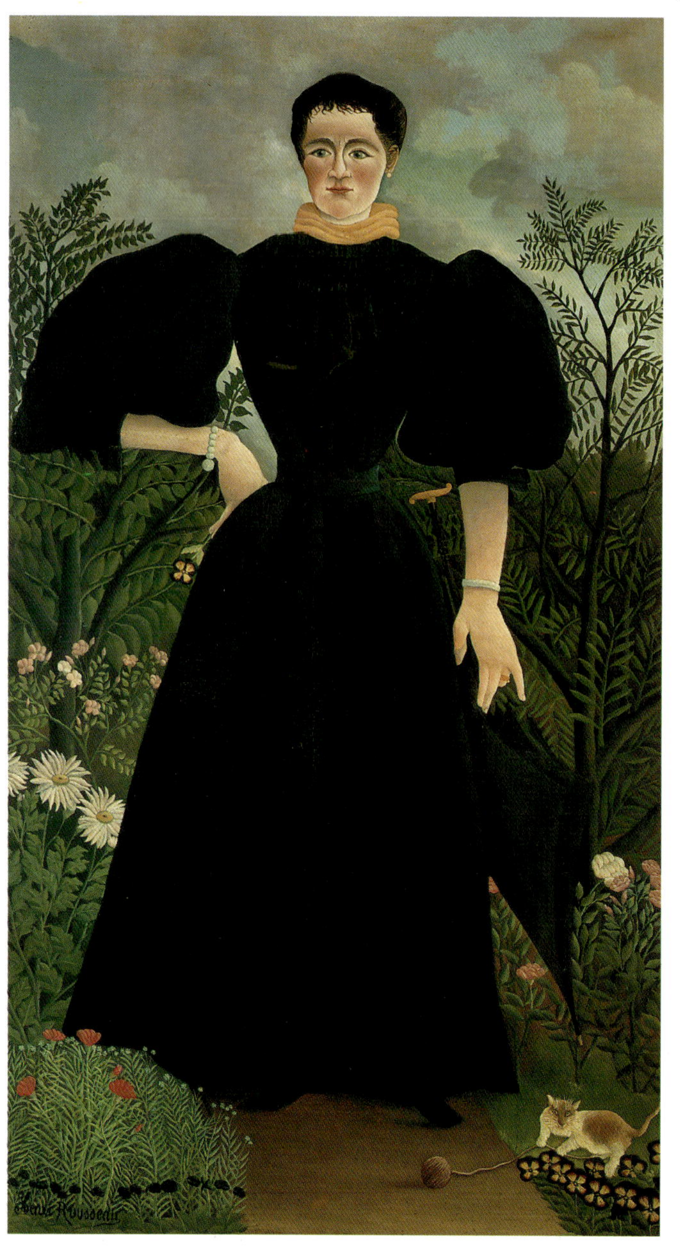

Henri Rousseau (1844-1910) is probably best known for the painting *The Storm in the Forest,* first exhibited in the Sale des Indépendants in 1891 under the title *Surprise!* It show a petrified tiger in a forest. Lions, tigers and jaguars appear regularly in his primitive work. Large cats were common themes at the time and appear in the exotic work of Delacroix and the North African painters Gerome and Fromentin. Rousseau also liked to slip cats into his domestic paintings. A serene tabby appears in Portrait of Edmond Frank (1906) and, in *Portrait of a Woman* completed in 1897, he slipped a tiny kitten playing with a ball of wool into the bottom righthand corner of the painting.

left *Henri Rousseau's* Portrait of a Woman – *1895-97.*

right Still Life with Cat and Mouse *from 1820 by an anonymous artist.*

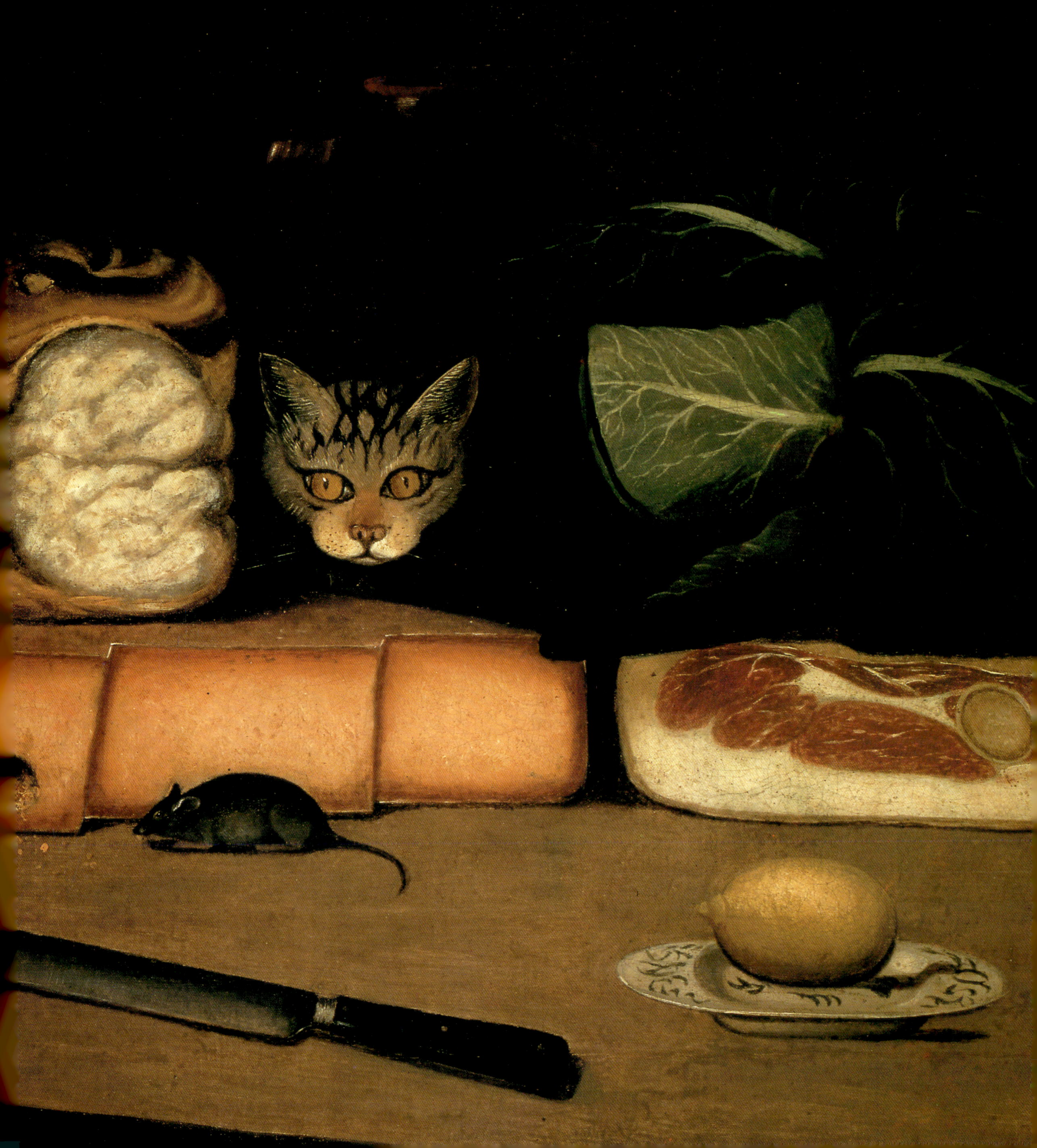

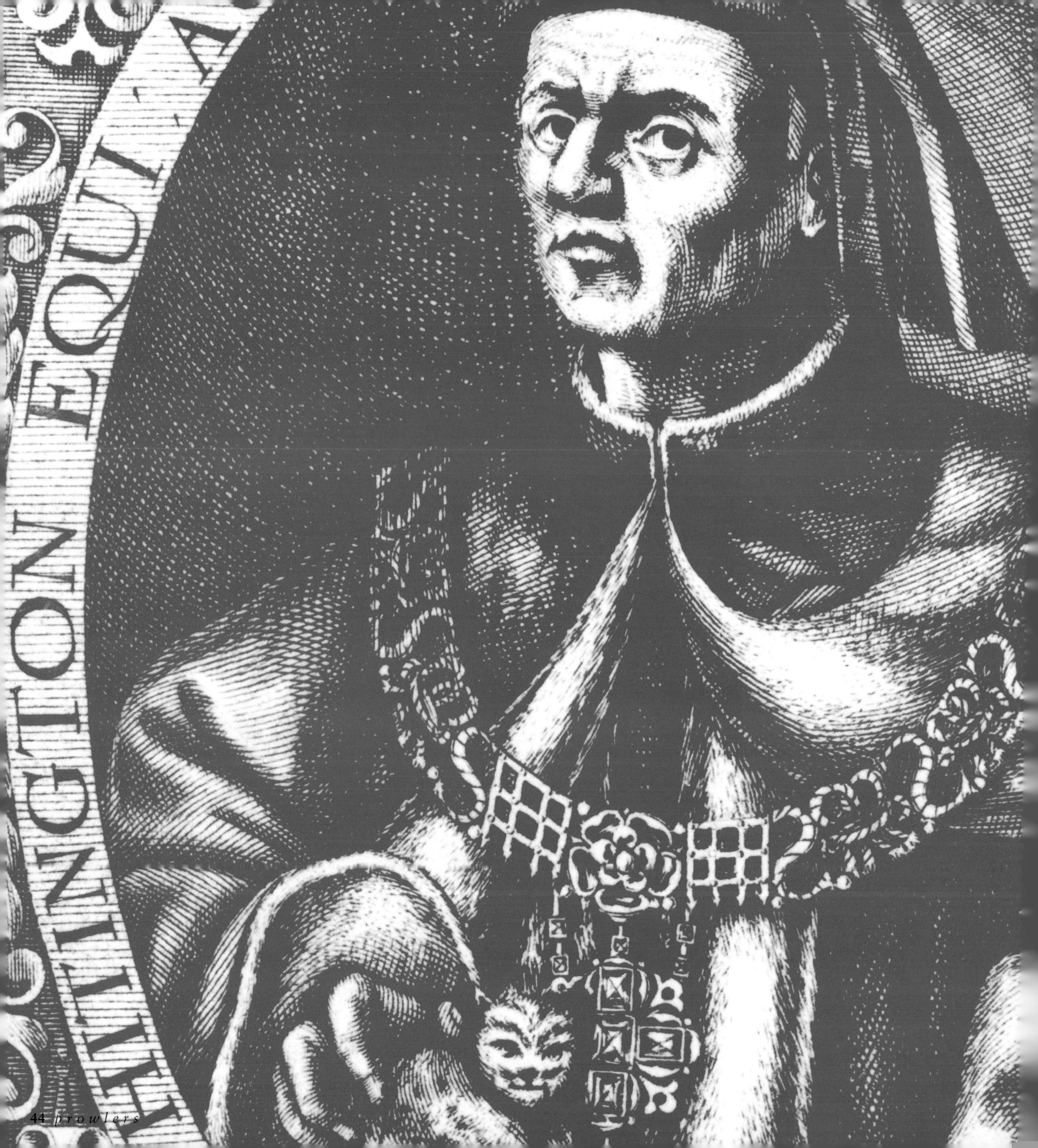

According to the traditional pantomime, the ten-year-old Dick Whittington possessed a cat. When he was an apprentice, Dick's employer took him on a voyage to Africa and he took his grimalkin with him. The King of Barbary's palace was infested with mice. He was so impressed by Dick's cat's prowess as a mouser, that he paid a huge sum for him. Dick returned to London and invested the money. This grew into a fortune and he became the Lord Mayor of London for three consecutive terms. At least, that is the legend.

The truth is that Dick Whittington was really the youngest son of Sir William Whittington of Pauntley in Gloucester. He did became one of the richest merchants in London thanks to cats – but not the feline variety. Cats were the name of the sailing barges used to bring coal to the city. He made large loans to his customers, which included Henry IV and Henry V, and bequeathed his fortune to charitable and public purposes. He did indeed serve as Lord Mayor of London for three terms: 1397-99, 1406-07 and 1419-20. However, he did not appear in pantomine until 1605.

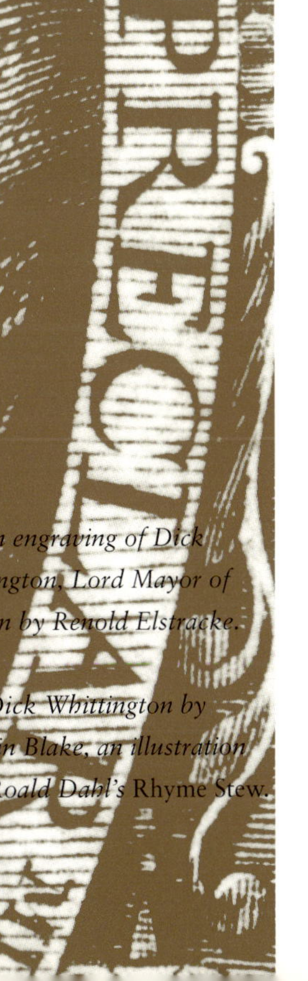

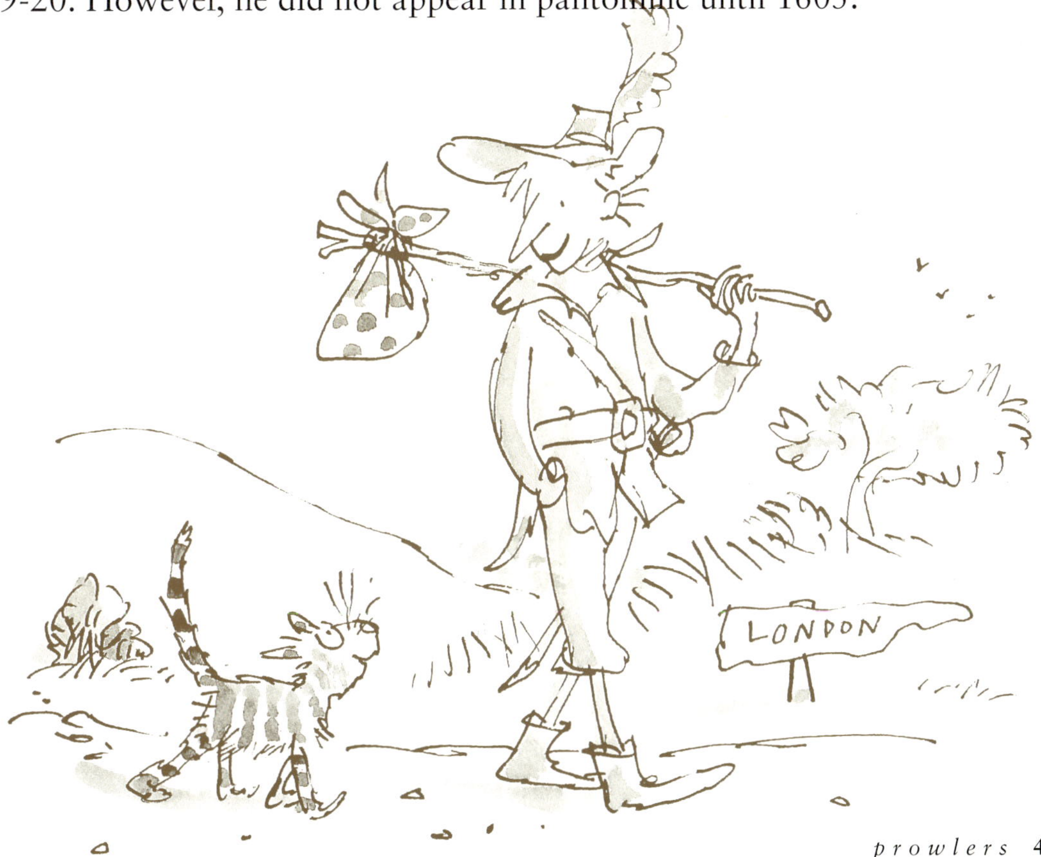

left *An engraving of Dick Whittington, Lord Mayor of London by Renold Elstracke.*

right *Dick Whittington by Quentin Blake, an illustration from Roald Dahl's* Rhyme Stew.

Given their undoubted courage, it is strange that cats are afraid of water. This anomaly was pointed out by naturalist Gilbert White in his *Natural History of Selborne:* 'There is a propensity belonging to common house-cats that is very remarkable; I mean their violent fondness for fish, which appears to be their favourite food: and yet nature in this instance seems to have planted in them an appetite that, unassisted, they know not how to gratify: for of all quadrupeds cats are the least disposed towards water; and will not, when they can avoid it, deign to wet a foot, much less to plunge into that element.'

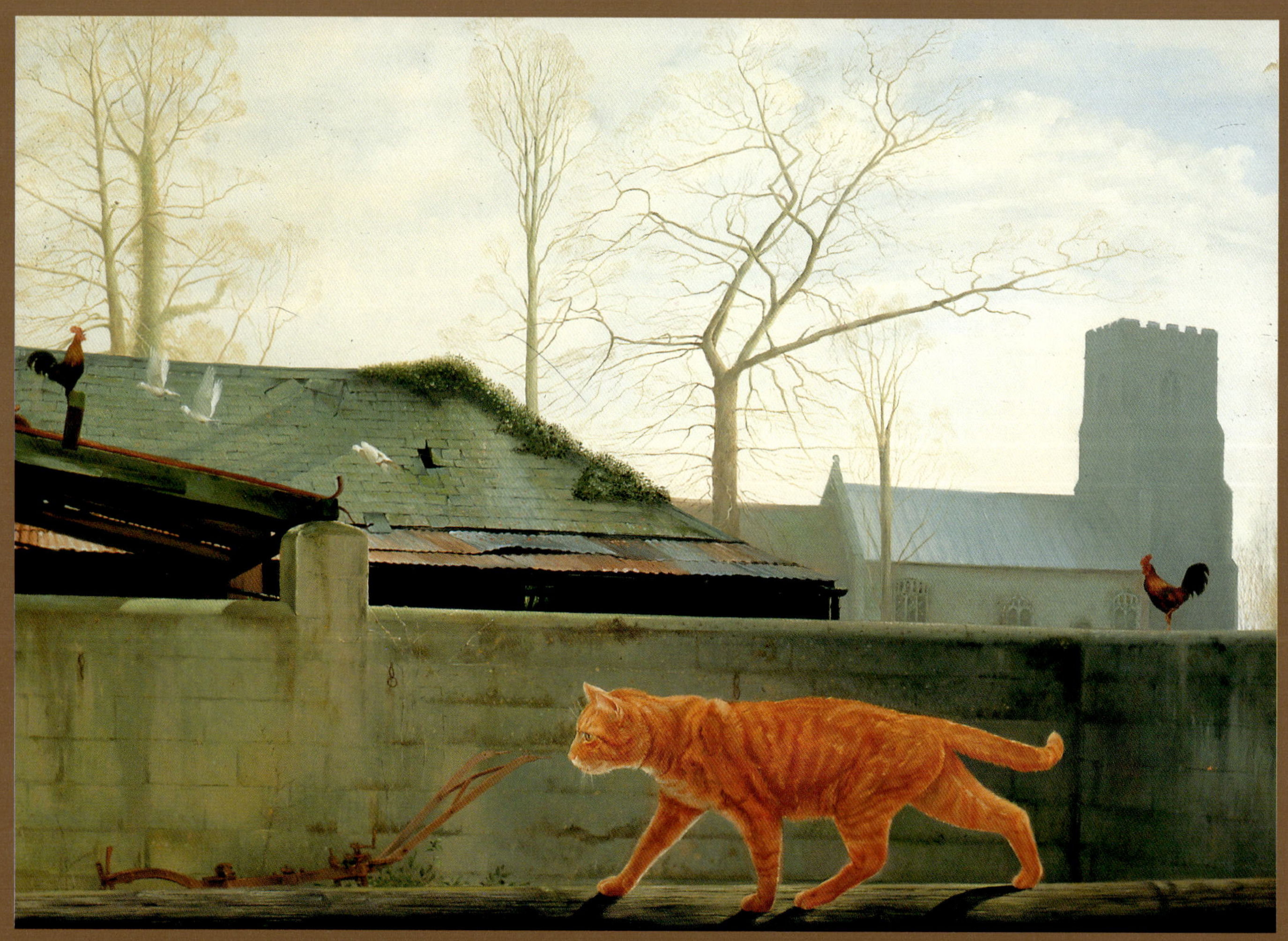

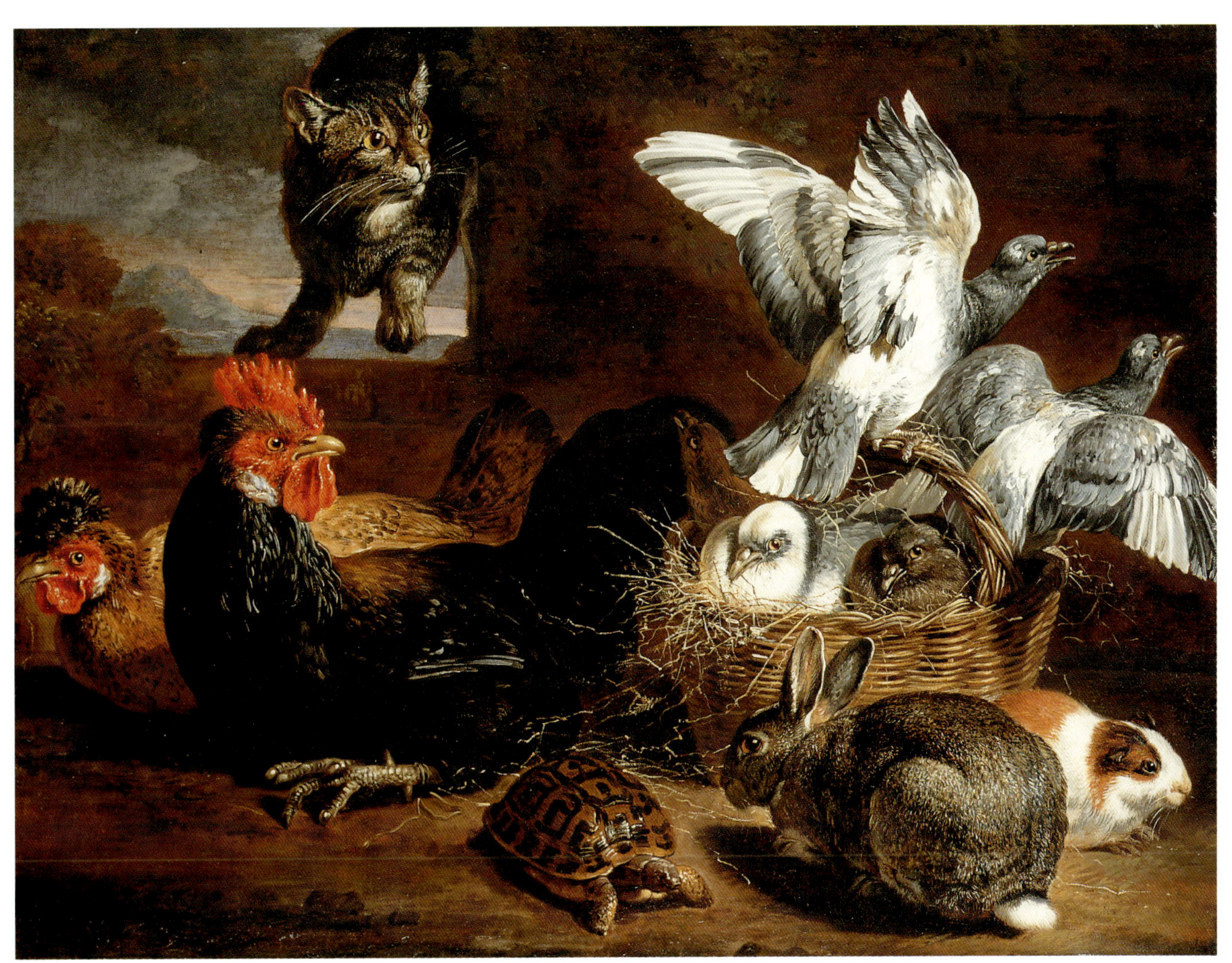

left Predators – *by 20th Century English artist Timothy Easton.*

above A Cat Stalking Pigeons in a Basket with Hens, a Rabbit, a Guinea Pig and a Tortoise *by David de Coninck – 1600s.*

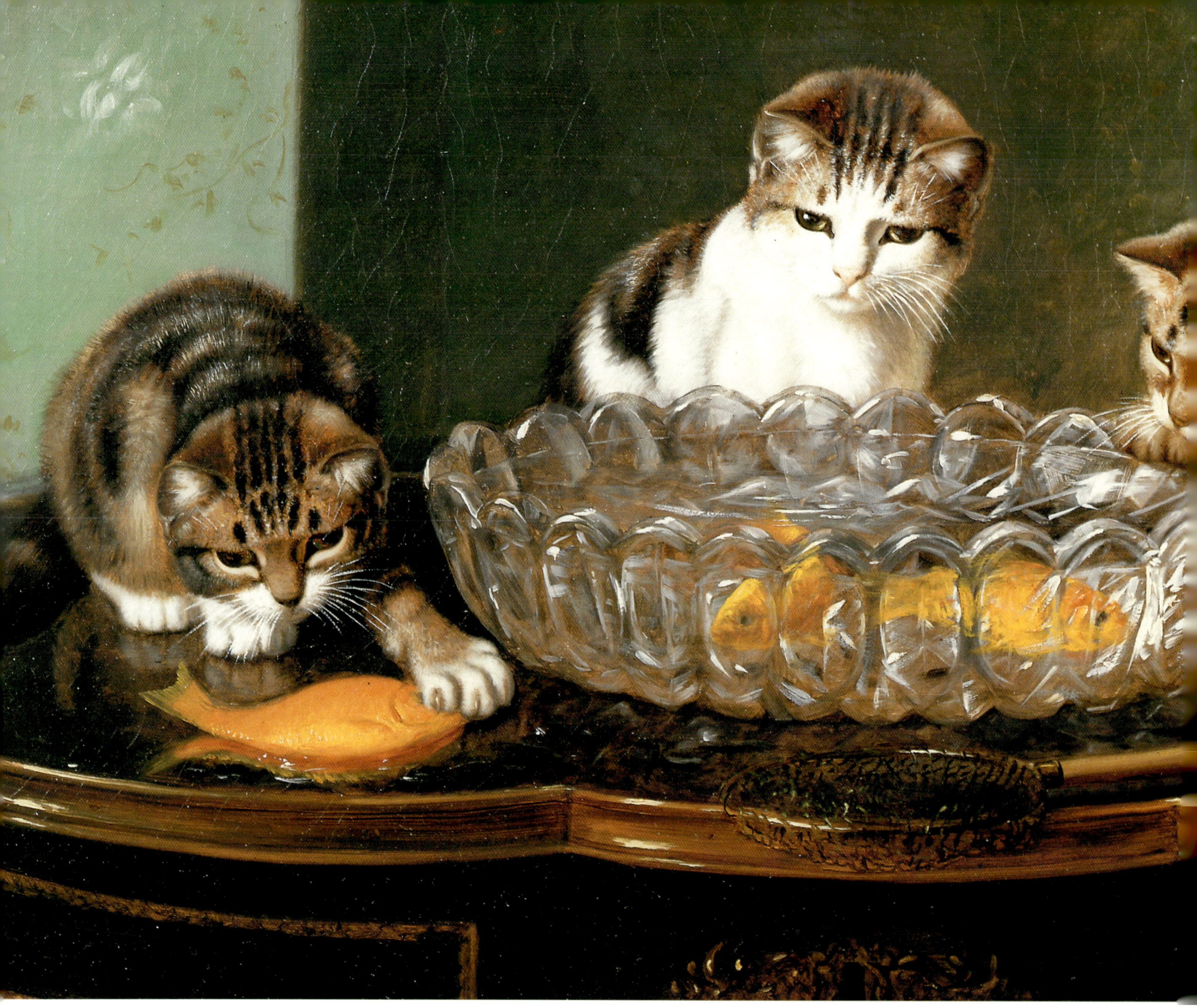

'all cats love fish,

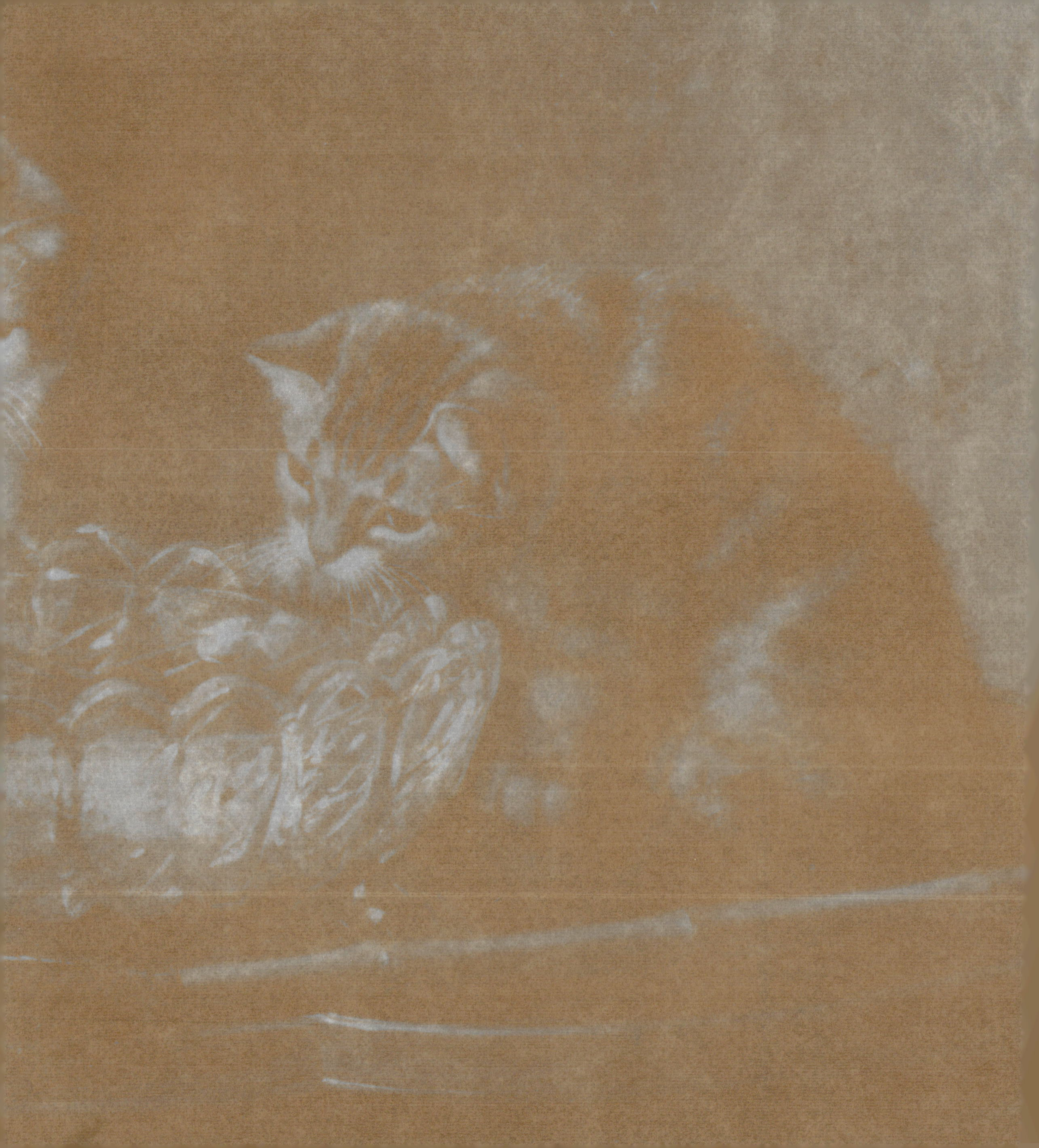

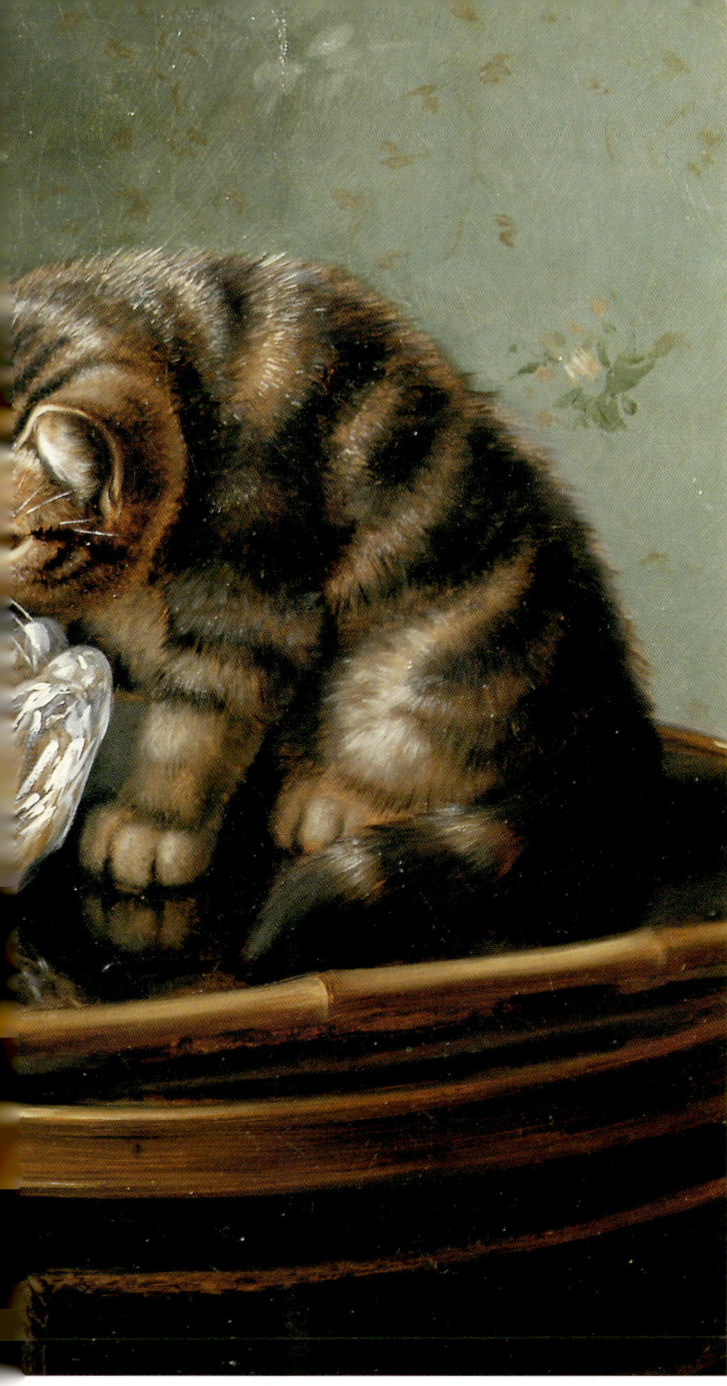

left The Fishing Party *by Horatio Henry Couldery – 19th Century.*

but fear to wet their paws'

5

pampered pets

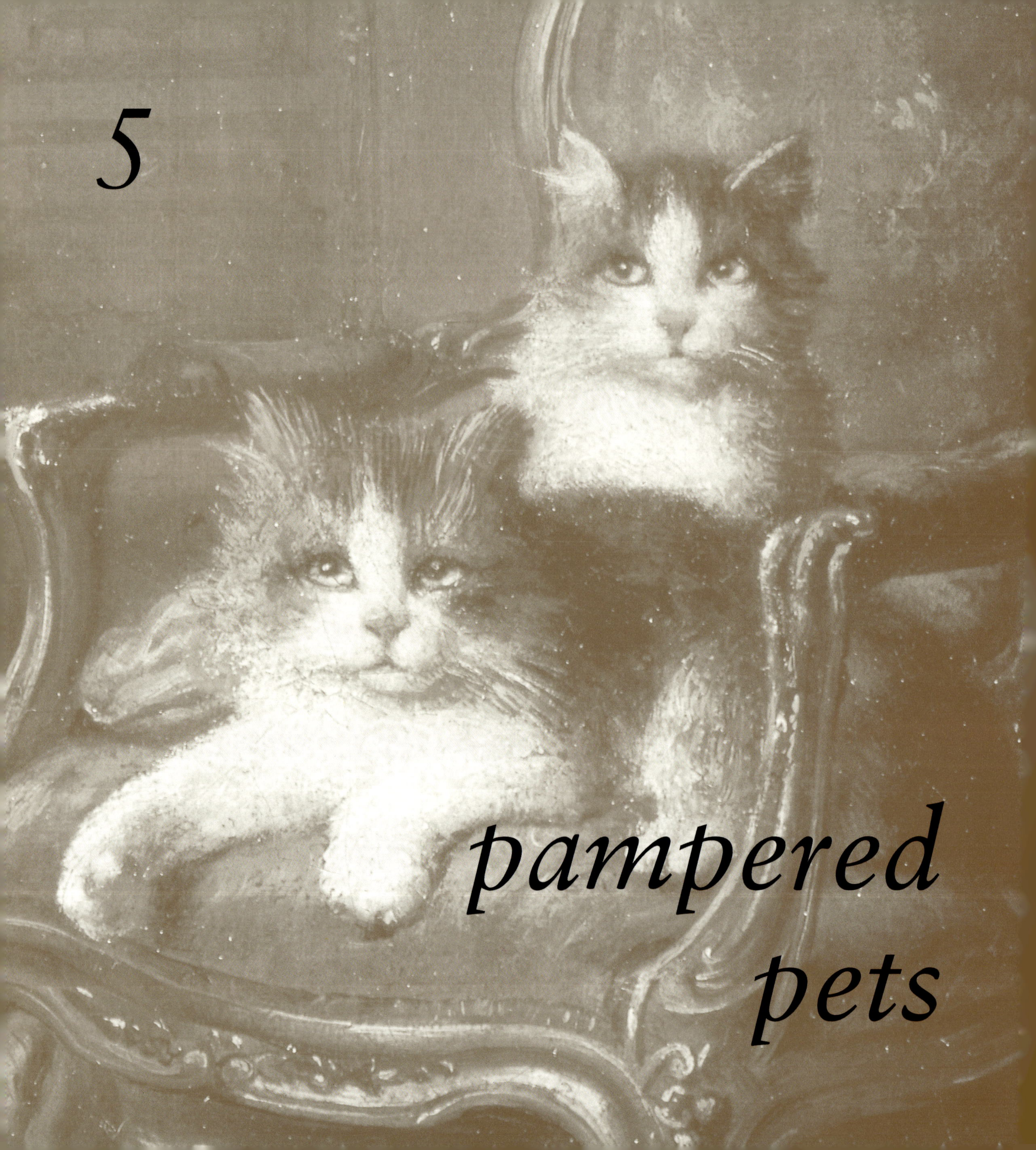

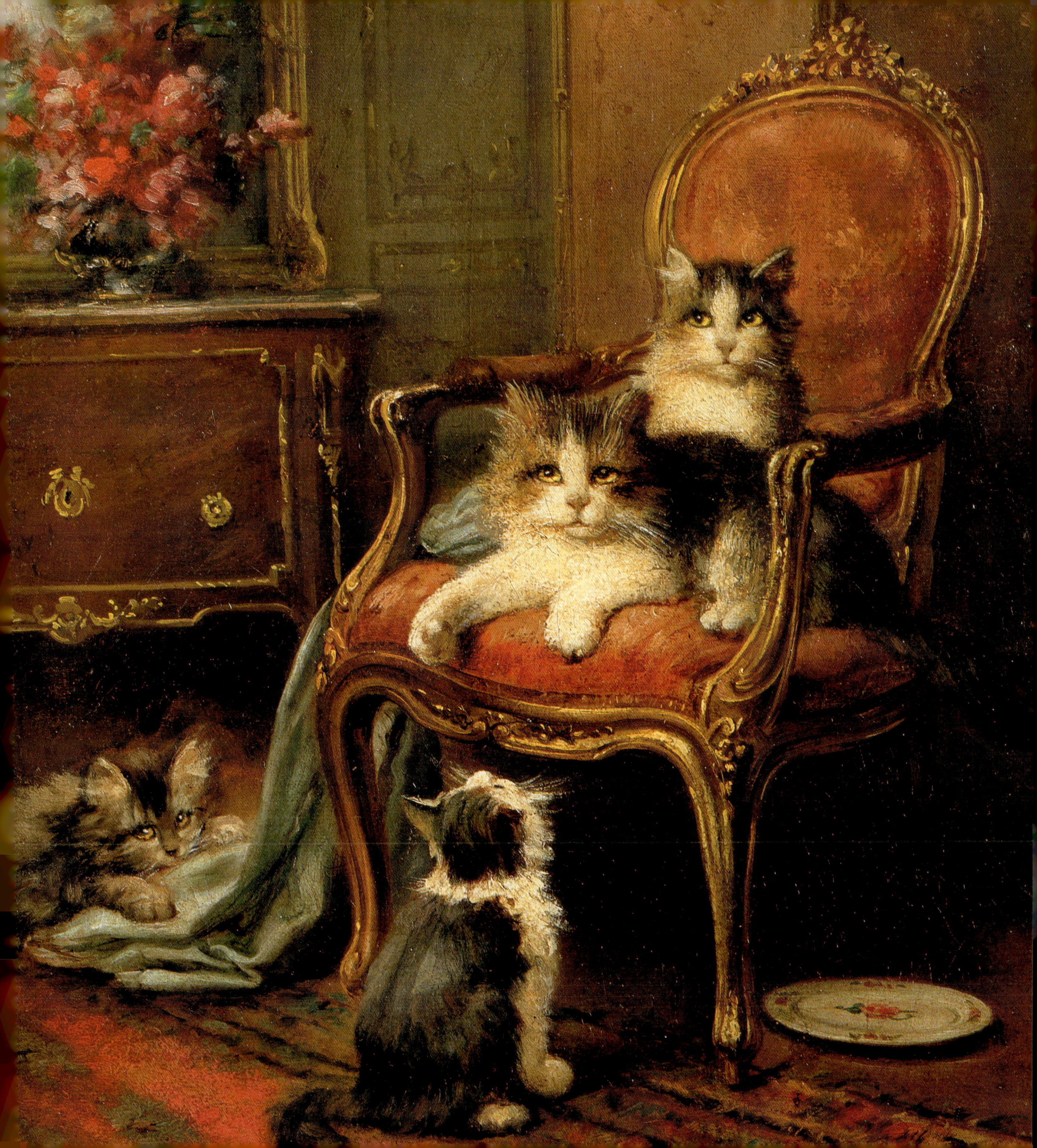

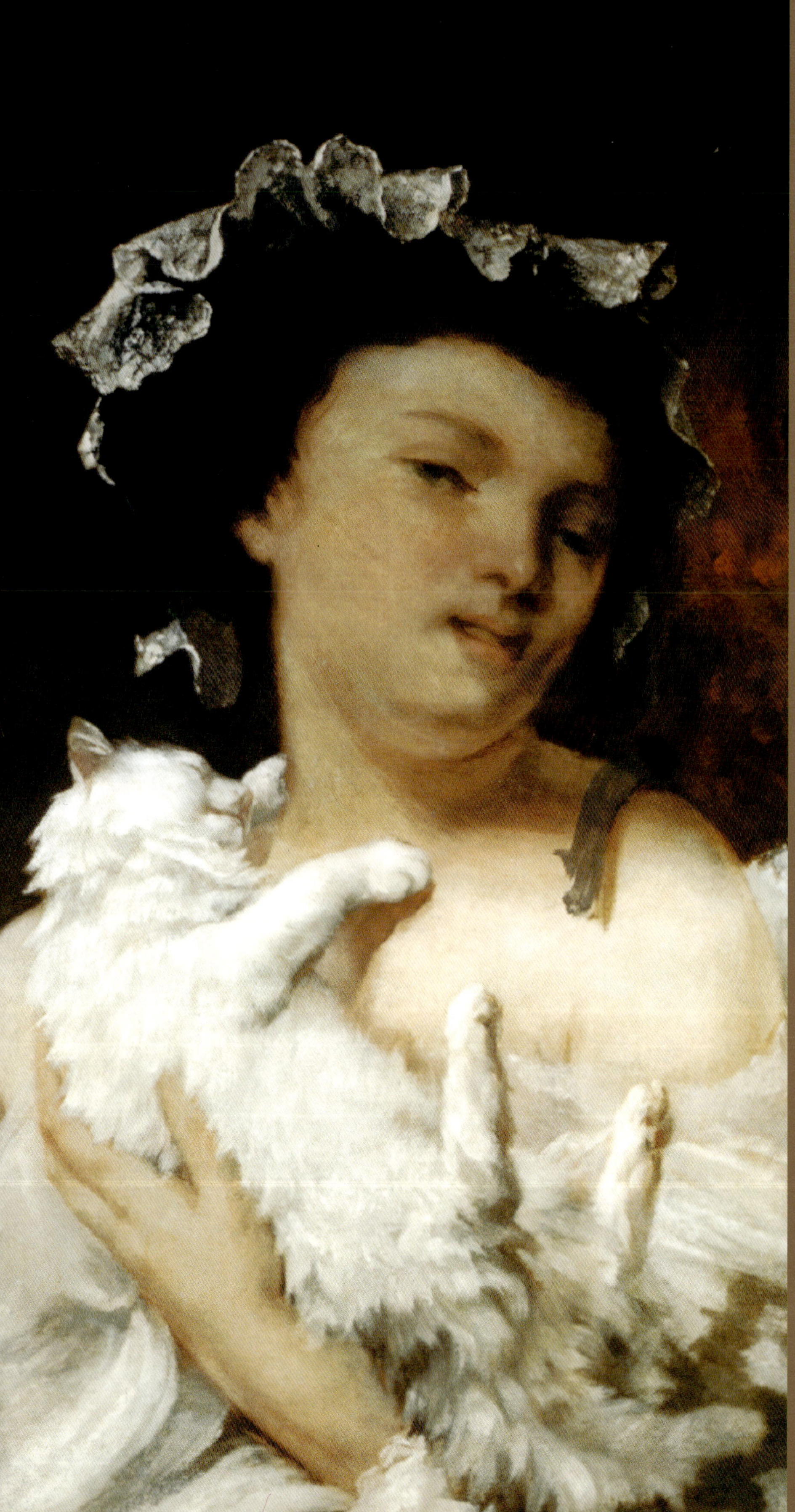

previous page The Favourite Chair *by Leon- Charles Huber – 1858-1928.*

Gustave Courbet (1819-1877) produced a series of paintings showing women with domestic pets. In 1866, he painting a supine nude with a parrot alighting on her outstretched hand and his *Woman with a Dog,* now in the Musee d'Orsay in Paris, is blatantly erotic. But his *Woman with a Cat* is altogether more subtle. This is was because he painted it in 1864, when the Salon jury had just rejected his *Venus Pursuing Psyche* on the grounds of indecency. Courbet remarked that if Venus and Psyche were immoral, then all the museums of Italy, France, and Spain would have to be closed. He struck back with *Woman with a Cat.* The woman in it is clothed but dishabille with only her shoulders naked. The cat, clutched to her chest, is plainly in a state of ecstatic abandonment, whose pleasure is echoed by the lascivious expression on the woman's face. Although there was nothing overtly objectional about the painting, there is an implied contempt for the Second Empire's tastes in eroticism and propriety.

left *Courbet's* Woman with a Cat – *1864.*

The 'Mistress of Montmartre' Suzanne Valadon (1865-1938) owed a debt to a cat, which she paid back in full. When she came to Paris as a young girl, she became a star of the artist's cabaret Le Chat Noir, which was named after the Edgar Allan Poe story. There she met the artists who made her famous as a model and taught her to paint. One of Le Chat Noir's denizens was Miguel Utrillo, the father of her son, the famous artist Maurice Utrillo.

The middle-class people from all over Paris were drawn to Le Chat Noir for a glimpse into the bohemian life of artists. Suzanne Valadon caused a sensation – and made a name for herself – when she slid down the banisters wearing only a mask. A newspaper printed by the cabaret, also called *Le Chat Noir,* brought her fame to a wider audience. In later life, when she became wealthy, she fed her cat Raminou on caviar; her dogs got fillet steak. Raminou was pampered and had the run of her household. Valadon painted Raminou on the bed, on sofas, cushions, tables and sitting on the lap of her housekeeper Lily Walton.

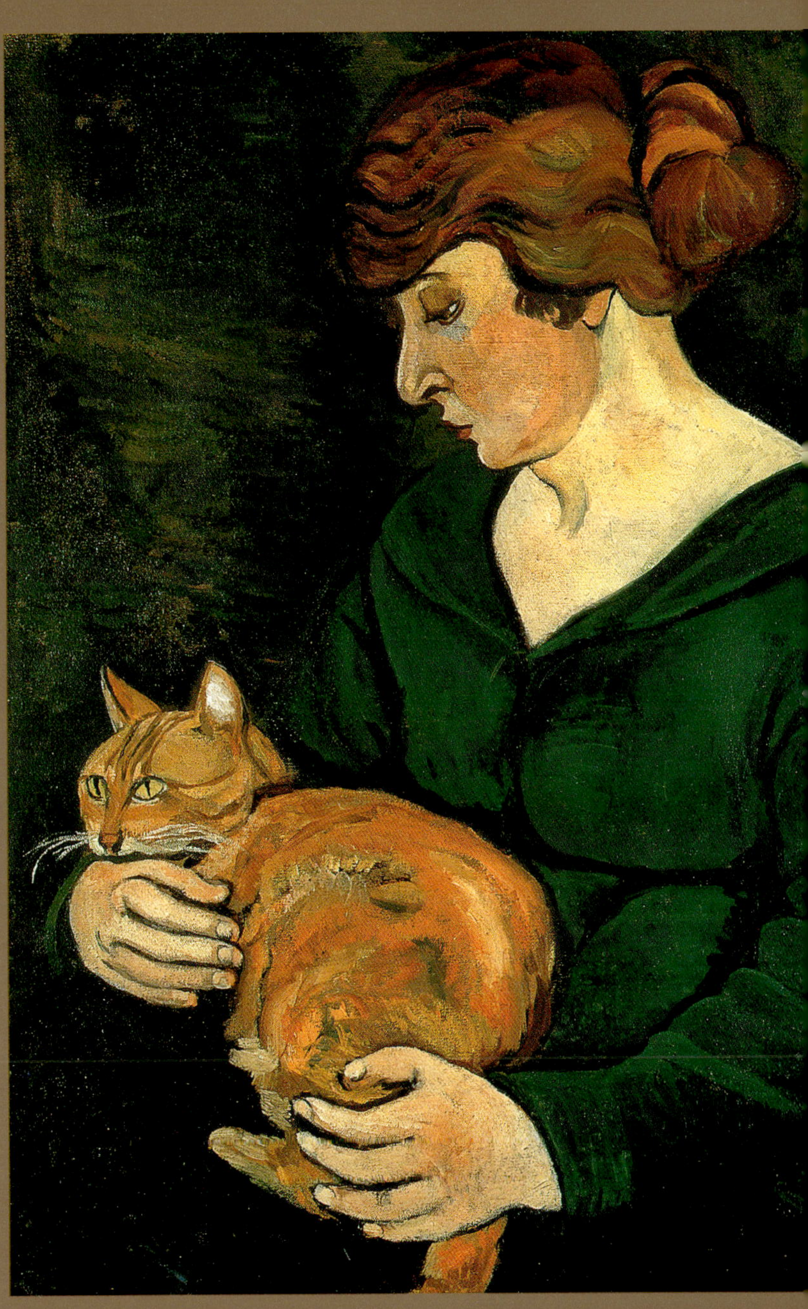

above *One of Suzanne Valadon's paintings of her cat. From 1920 this one is called* Louison et Raminov.

Dr Dowing, a friend of the 18th century English humanist philosoper Jeremy Bentham, wrote of the great man's love of cats:

'Bentham was very fond of animals, particularly "pussies", as he called them, when they had domestic virtues, but he had no particular affection for the common race of cats. He had one, however, of which he used to boast that he had "made a man of him", and whom he was wont to invite to eat macaroni at his own table. This puss got knighted, and rejoiced in the name of Sir John Langbourne. In his early days, he was a frisky, inconsiderate, and, to say the truth, somewhat profligate gentleman; and had, according to his patron, the habit of seducing light and giddy young ladies, of his own race, into garden of Queen's Square Place; but tired at last, like Solomon, of pleasures and vanities, he became sedate and thoughtful – took to the church, laid down his knightly title, and was installed as the Reverend John Langbourne. He gradually obtained a great reputation for sanctity and learning, and a Doctor's degree was conferred upon him. When I knew him, in his declining days, he bore no other name than the Reverend Doctor John Lanbourne: and he was alike conspicuous for his gravity and philosophy. Great respect was invariably shown his reverence: and it was supposed that he was not far off from a mitre, when old age interfered with his hopes and honours. He departed amidst the regrets of his many friends, and was gathered to his fathers, and to eternal rest, in a cemetery in Milton's garden.

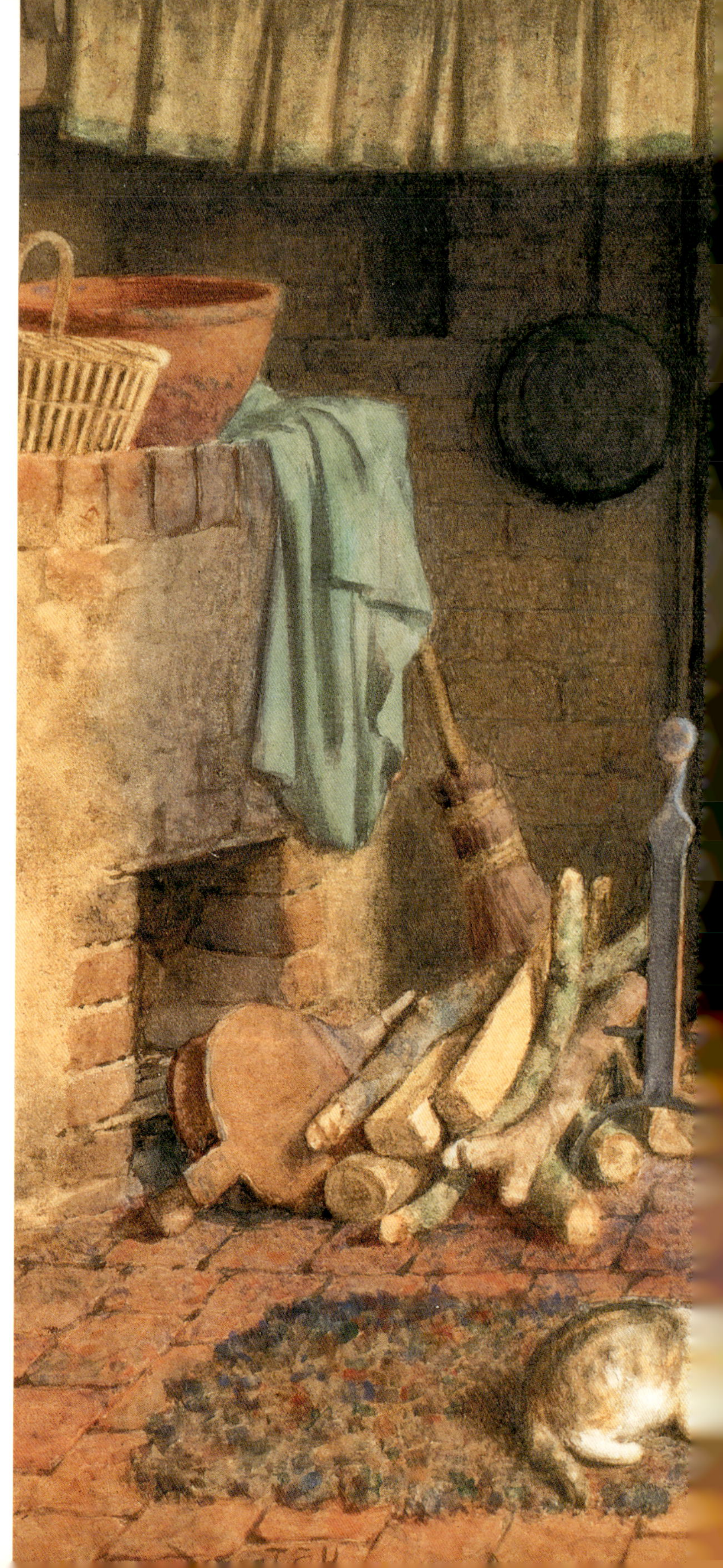

right By the Fireside *by Henry Spernon Tozer – 1892.*

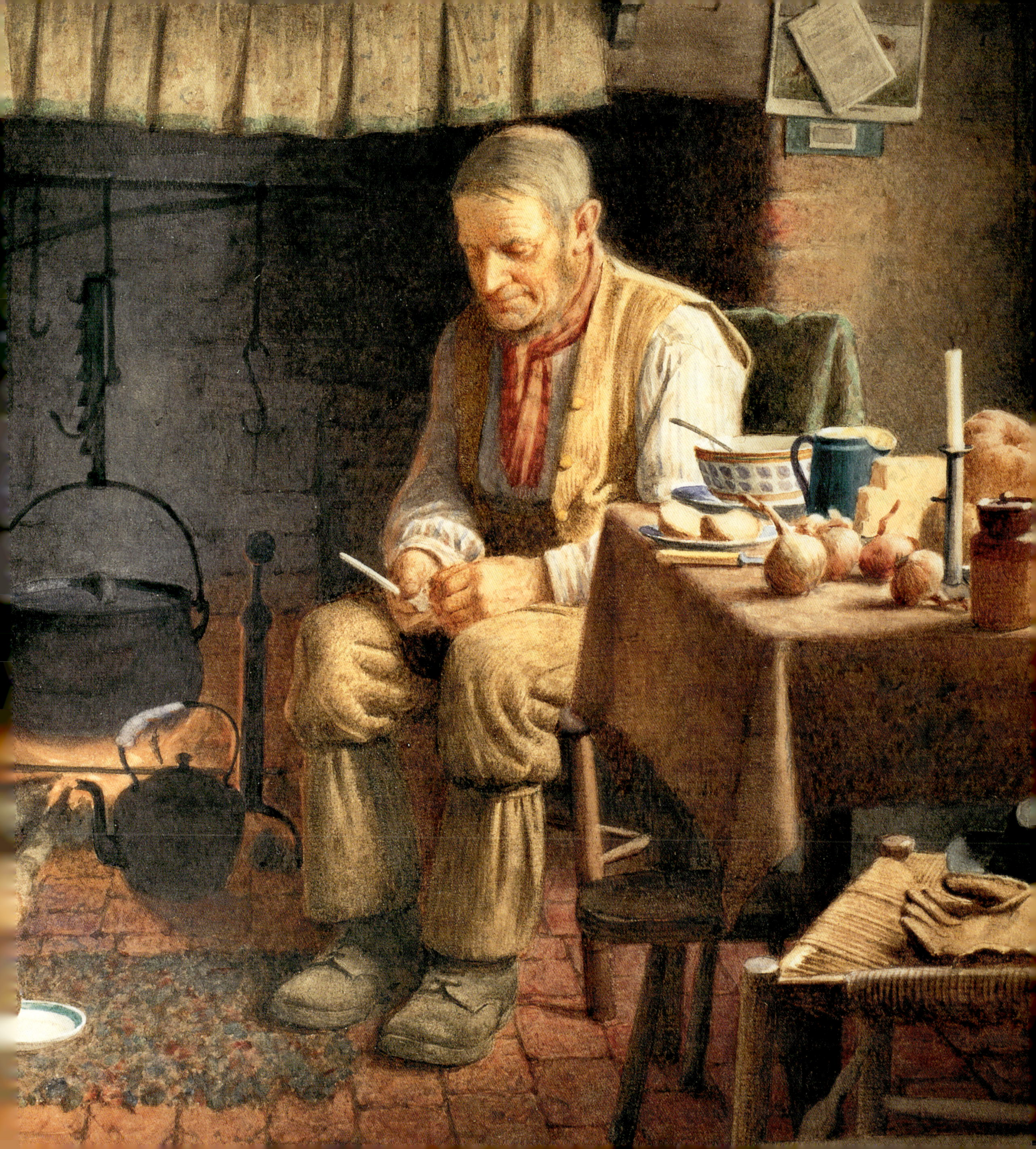

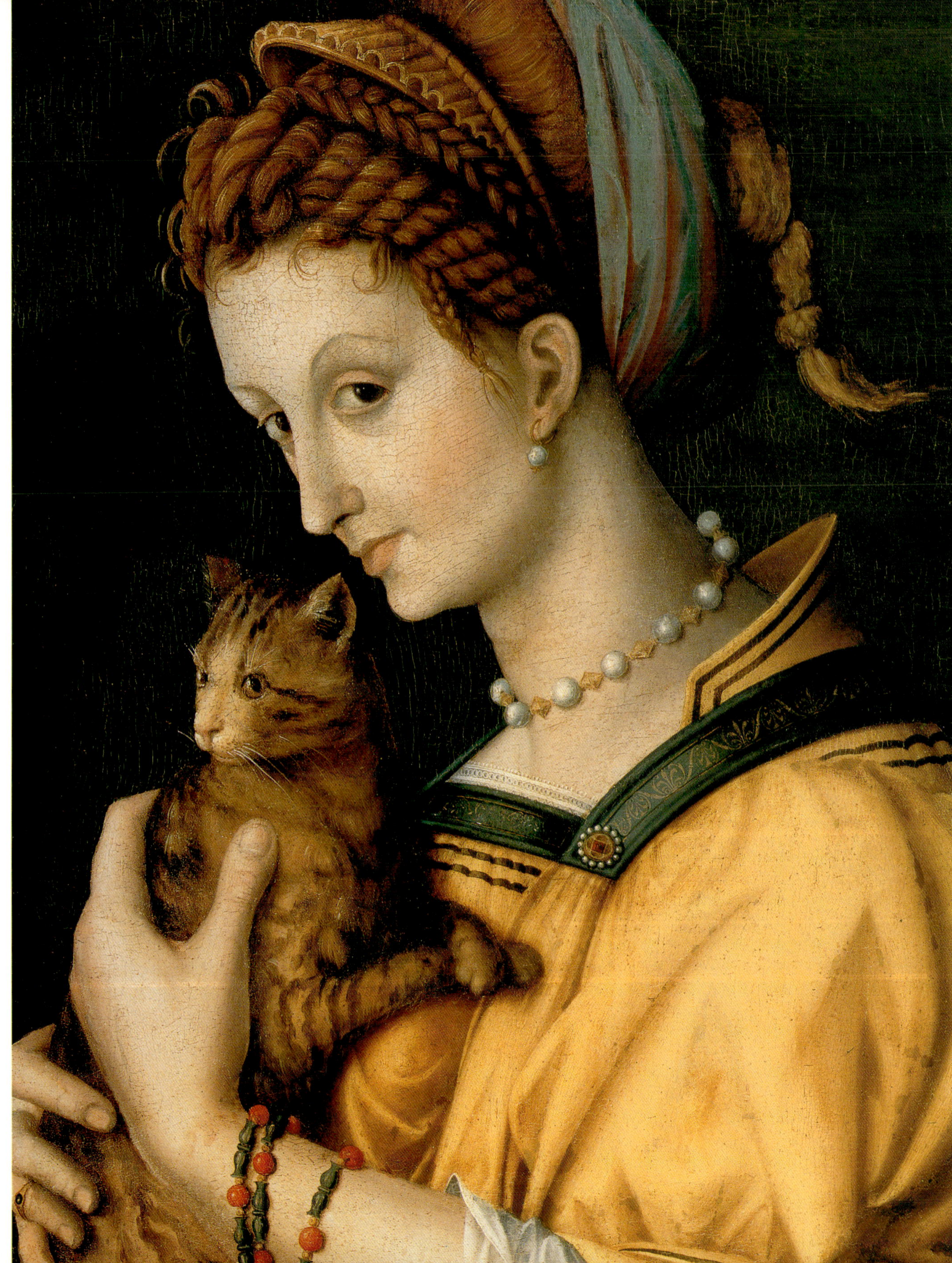

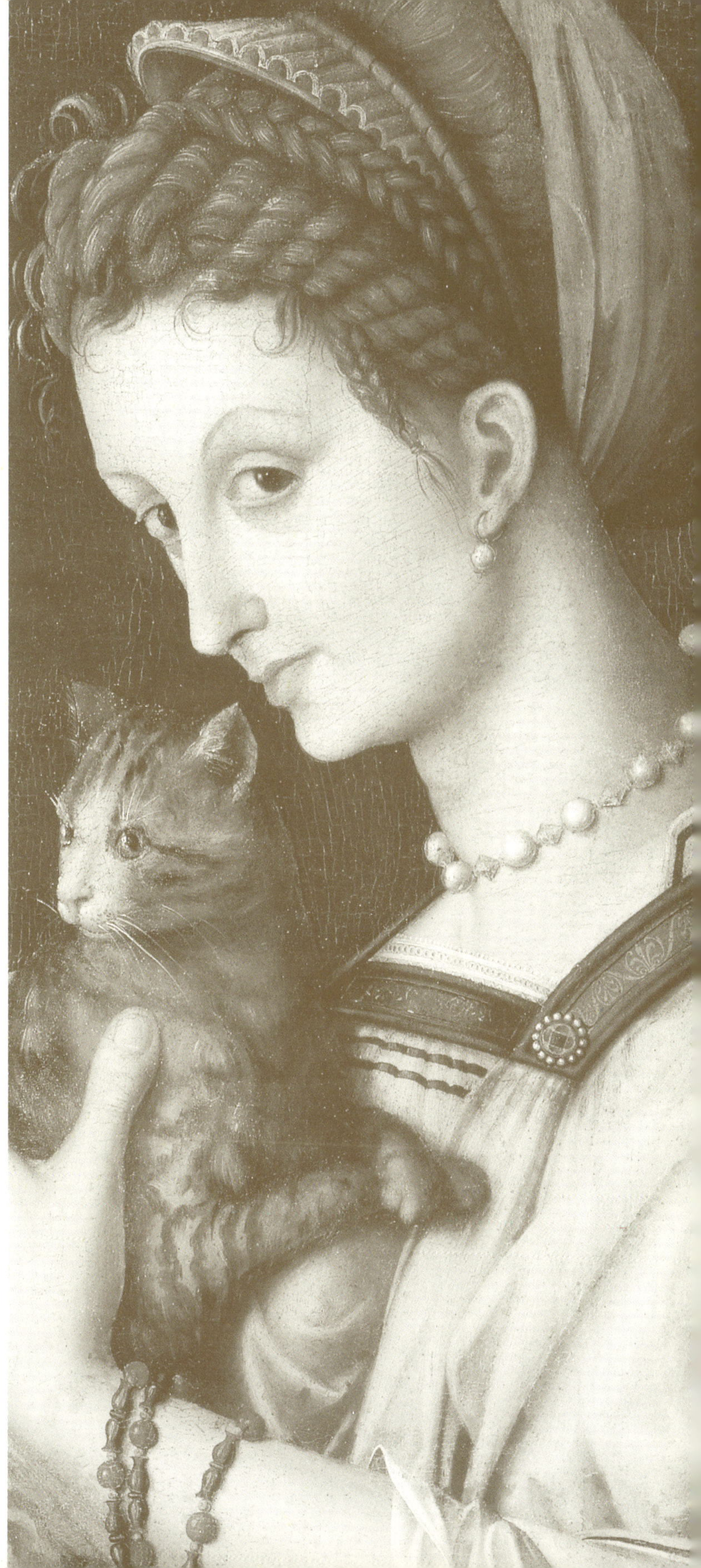

left Lady with a Cat *by Francesco Ubertini Il Bacchiacca from the Italian Renaissamce.*

Although their output was hugely dominated – and characterised in the modern public mind – by religious art, the painters of the Italian Renaissance in fact dealt with a great many other subject areas, particularly portraits of the nobility, their families and – as in the case of Bacchiacca's *Lady with a Cat* – their pets. Francesco Ubertini Il Bacchiacca (1494–1557) is thought to have been a pupil of Pietro Vannuci Perugino whose monumental work is best represented by a fresco series commissioned for the Sistine Chapel. Nevertheless Bacchiacca went on to develop his own eclectic style, influenced by his fellow Florentine artist 'the faultless painter' Andrea del Sarto. The *Lady with a Cat*'s languid looks are typical of Renaissance artists' image of gentlewomen.

Dr Johnson, the British lexicographer, defined a cat in his, the first, English dictionary as: 'A domestick animal that catches mice, commonly reckoned by naturalists the lowest order of the leonine species.' In fact, he had a great affection for his cat which was called Hodge. Johnson's friend James Boswell wrote in his Life of Dr Johnson:

'I will never forget the indulgence with which Dr Johnson treated his cat, Hodge, for who himself used to go out and buy oysters lest the servants, having that trouble, should take a dislike to the poor creature. I am unluckily one of those who have an antipathy to cats, so that I am uneasy when in the room with one, and I own I frequently suffered a good deal from the presence of the same Hodge. I remember him one day scrambling up Dr Johnson's breast apparently with much satisfaction while my friend, smiling and half-whistling, rubbed down his back and pulled him by the tail and when I observed he was a fine cat, saying, "Why yes, sir, but I have had cats that I like better then this," and then, as if perceiving Hodge to be out of countenance, adding, "but he is a very fine cat, a very fine cat indeed."'

right *A truly pampered pet,* The Cat's Lunch *by the 18th/19th Century French artist Margueritte Gerard.*

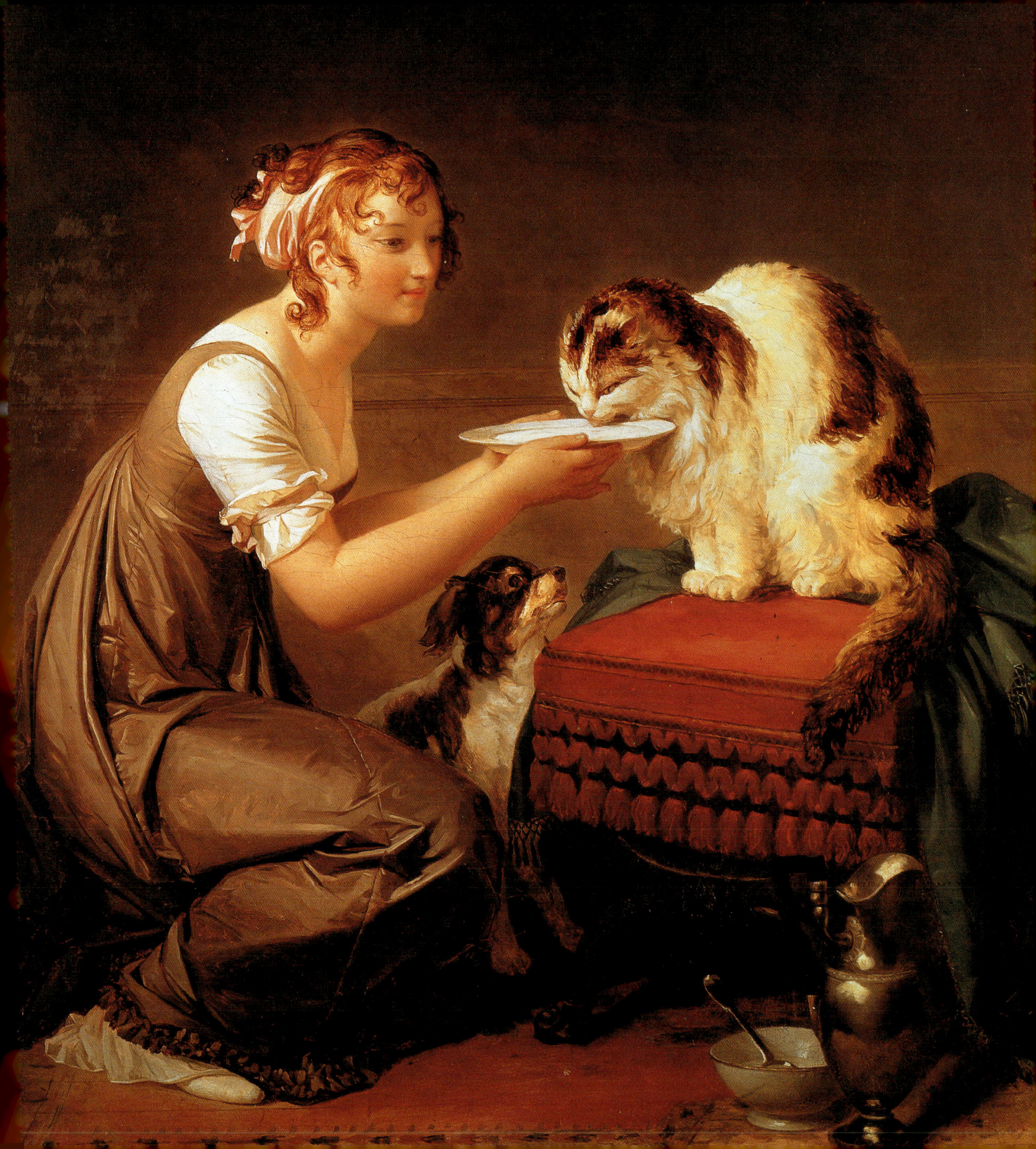

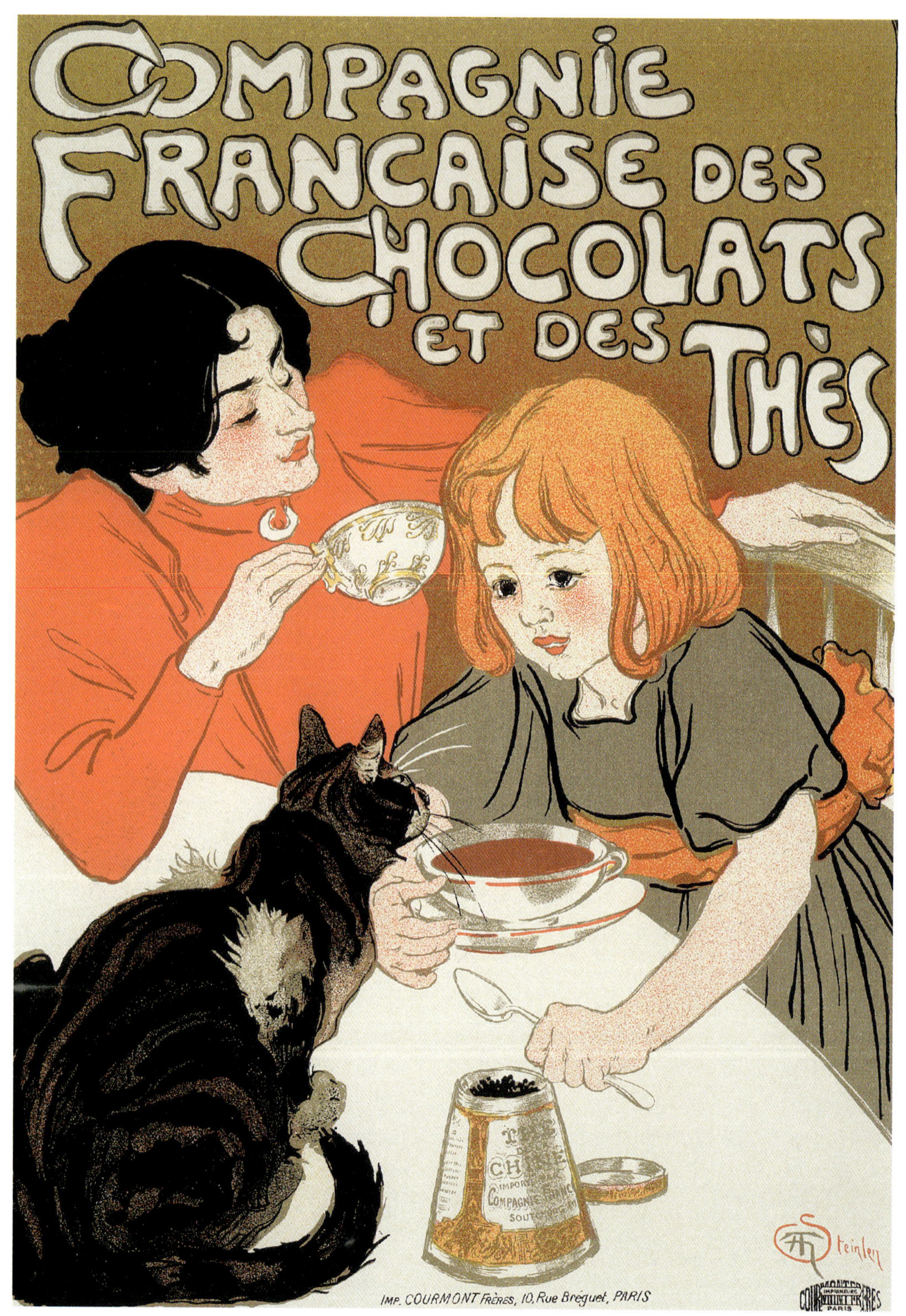
COMPAGNIE
FRANCAISE DES
CHOCOLATS
ET DES THÈS
Steinlen
IMP. COURMONT Frères, 10, Rue Bréguet, PARIS

Theophile-Alexandre Steinlen (1859-1923) was a French graphic artist who was devoted to cats and drew them throughout his long career. He lived in Paris and his models were the habitues of the rooftops, gutters, cemeteries and garbage bins of the Butte de Montmartre district. They belonged to seamstresses, concierges and fellow artists. As well as thousands of drawings, paintings and lithographs of cat, Steinlen also modelled them in wax and cast them in bronze. His poster for the Compagnie Francais des Chocolats et des Thes was made around 1899. While the human figures in the lithograph are sparse and flat, owing a lot to Henri de Toulouse-Lautrec (1864-1901) in their rendition, the tortoiseshell cat is detailed and fully formed. It is only too clear where the artist's interest lies. The bright colours of the rest of the poster are anchored by the dark colour of the cat which draws the eye to the table. As for the cat, it only too clear that its interest lies in the little girl's bowl of chocolate.

Toulouse-Lautrec created many similar posters, but usually featuring his favourite subjects – singers, dancers, circus performers and horse-back riders. However, at the height of his career, he produced a poster advertising Mary Belfort. In it, the Irish singer is holding a black cat which makes a stark contrast with her bright red dress and reinforces the power of her raven black hair.

left *Steinlen's advertisement for the Compagnie Francais des Chocolats et des Thes.*

6

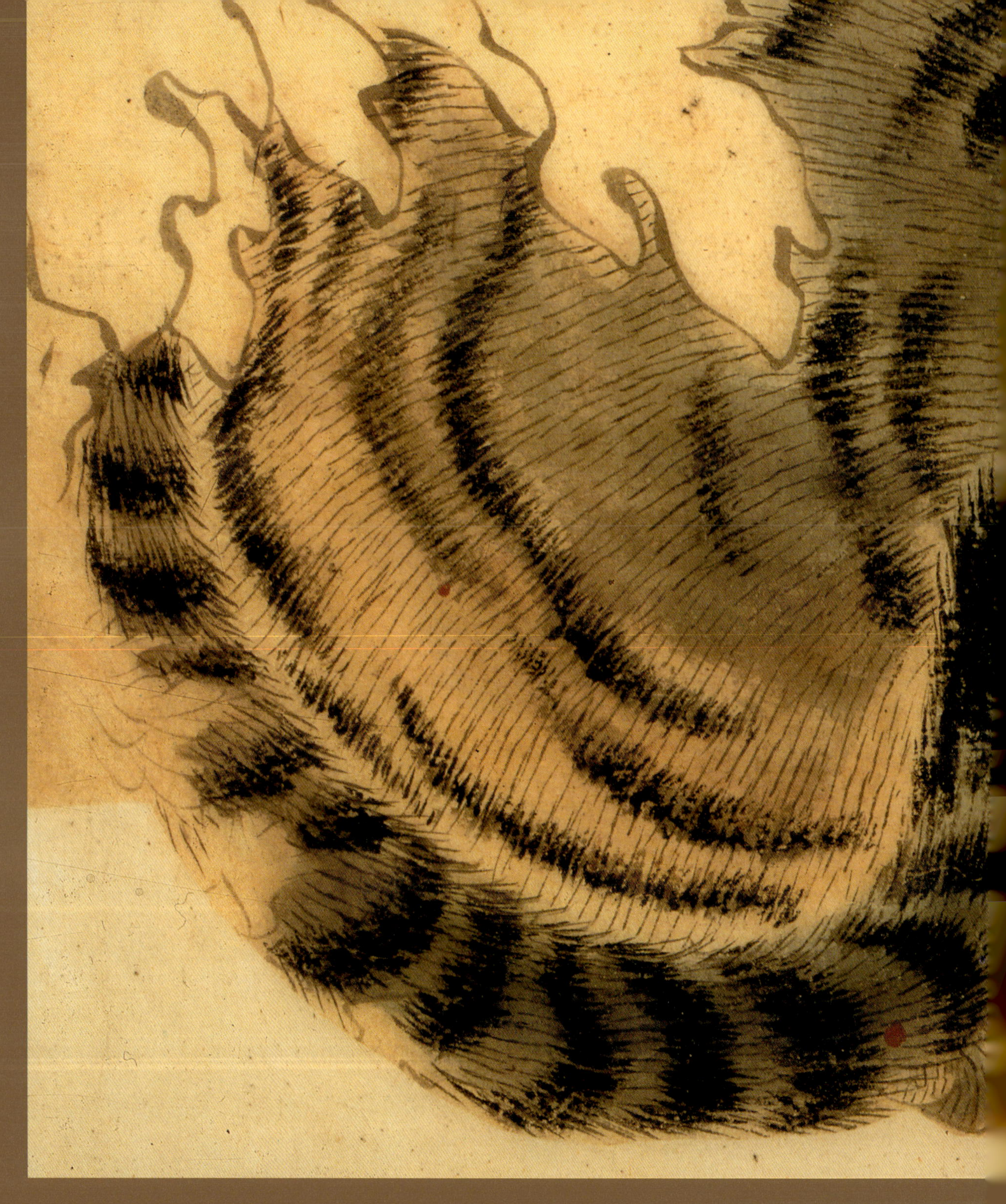

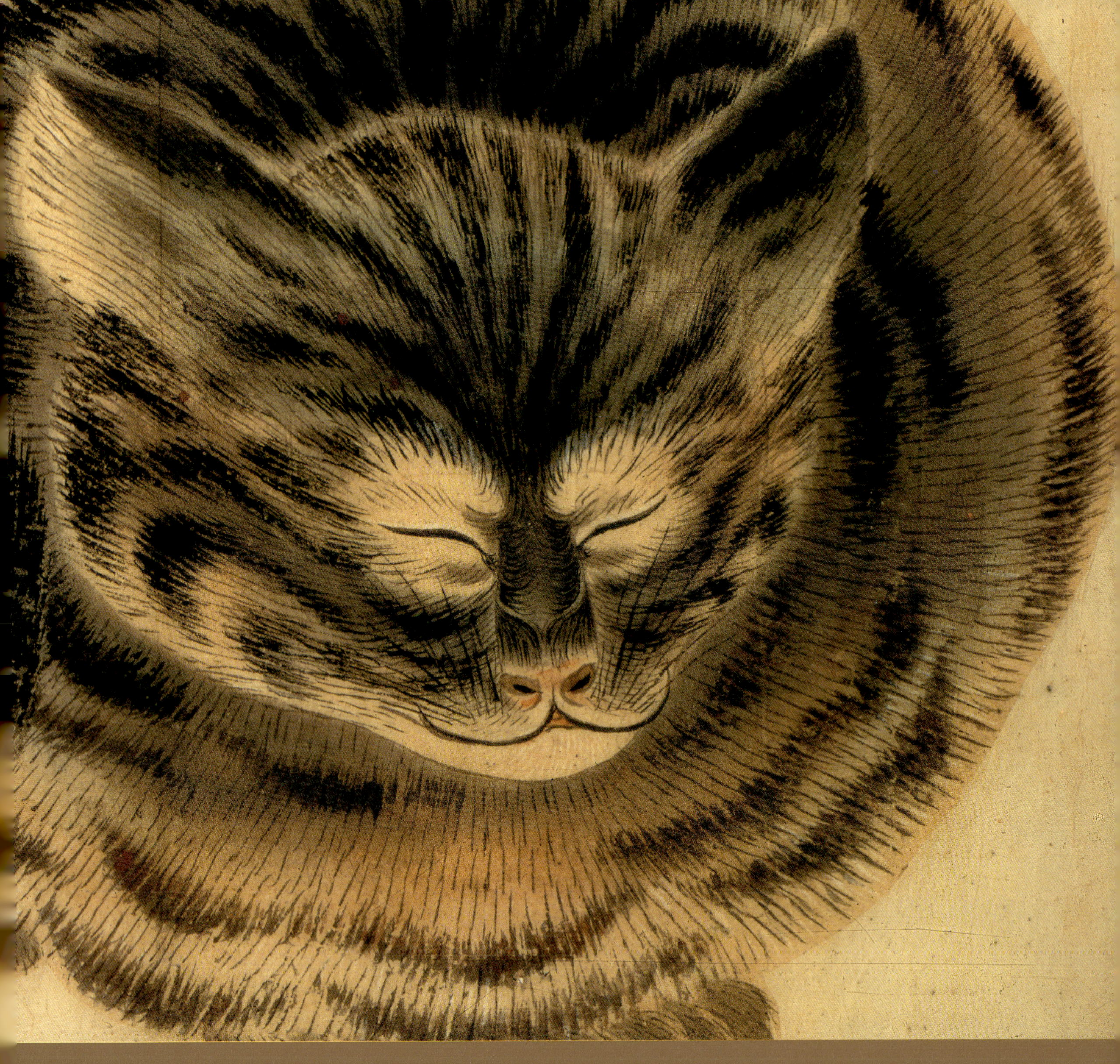

lazybones

Henriette Ronner-Knip (1821-1909) was a remarkable woman. She made a living from painting at a time when it was unheard of for a woman to do so. But she had little choice. She had learnt painting from her father, an established artist who suddenly went blind. In 1850, she married Feico Ronner, who then fell ill. So it was up to Henriette to provide for the family. Although she went on to become famous across Europe for her paintings of cats, Henriette Ronner-Knip's first major success was with a painting of dog. In *La mort d'un ami,* she showed a poor sand vendor crying over the body of his dog, which lies dead under his dogcart.

This sentimentality appears throughout her work. But with her cat paintings she is left the street behind. Her cats all came from wealthy homes.

Once she put an advertisement in the the newspaper for new models. Lower class women who turned up with cats of doubtful parentage were quickly shown the door. Her well-to-do customers expected nothing less. From her studio in Brussels, she turned out a seemingly endless series of cat paintings, charging up to 1500 guilders for a painting at a time when it was possible to live in comfort on 500 guilders a year.

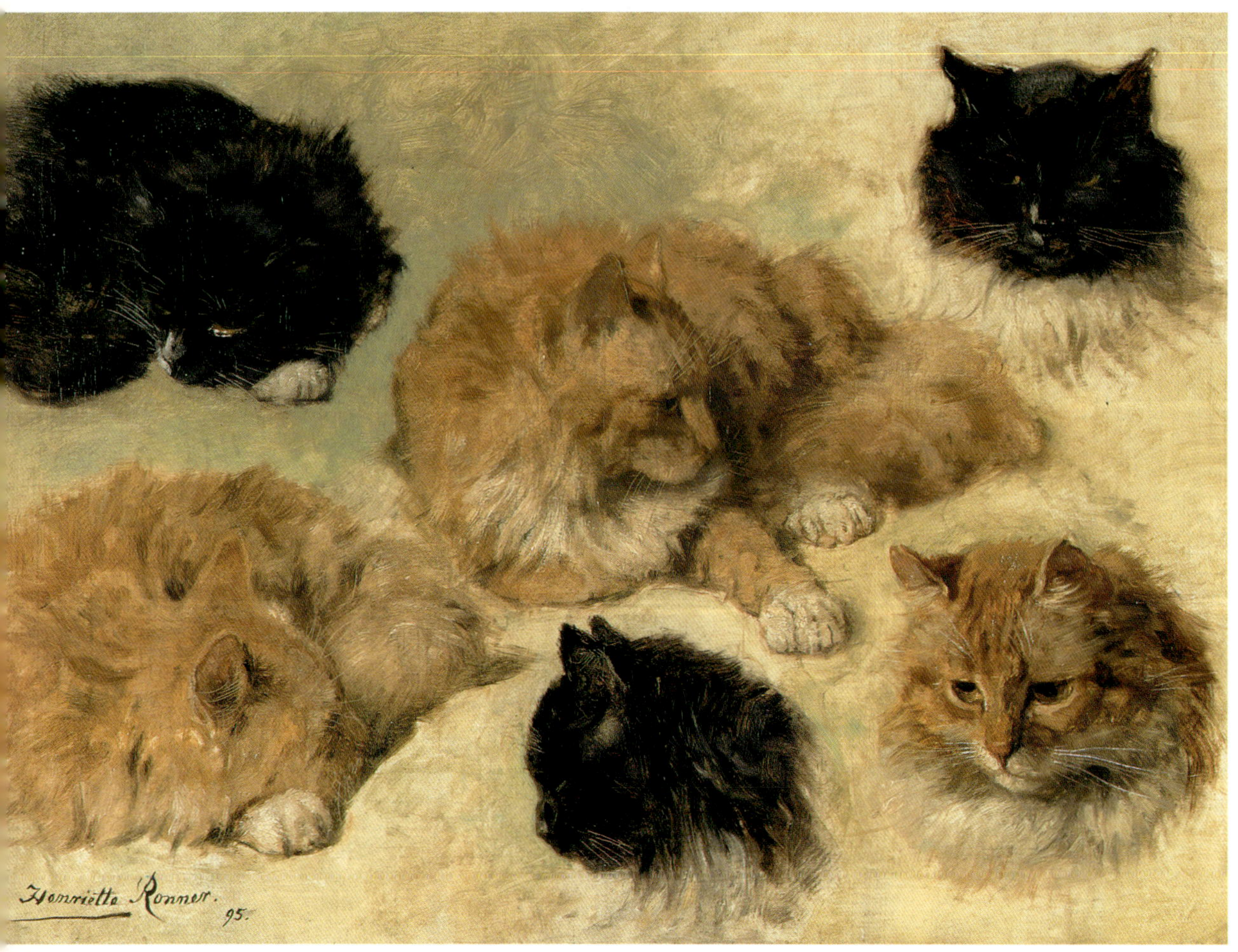

previous page *A perfectly relaxed and lazy image of a restful cat,* Sleeping Cat – *published 1850.*

left Studies of Cats, *by Henriette Ronner-Knip – 1895.*

right *Another of Ronner-Knip's numerous cat paintings –* Sitting Pretty.

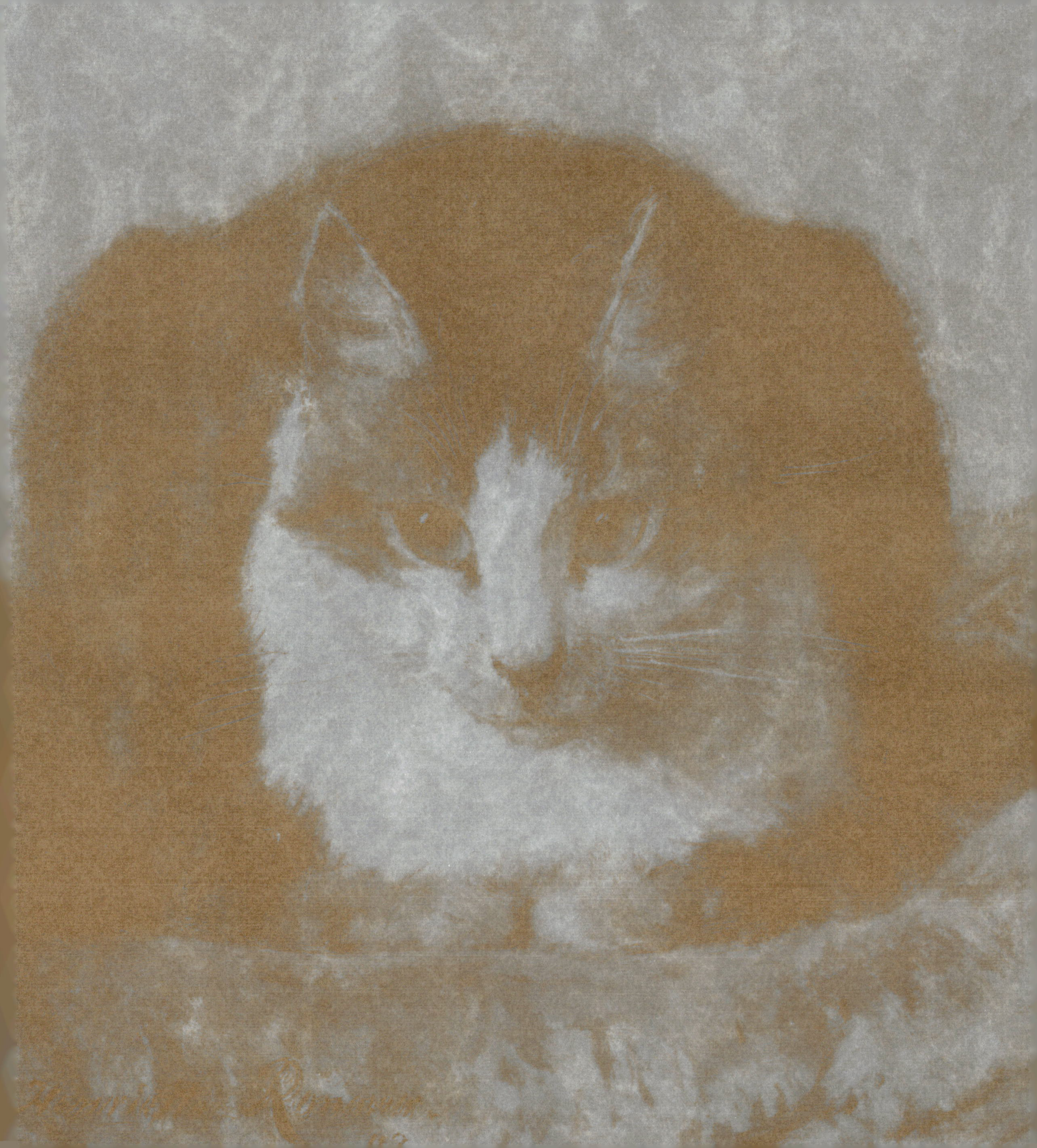

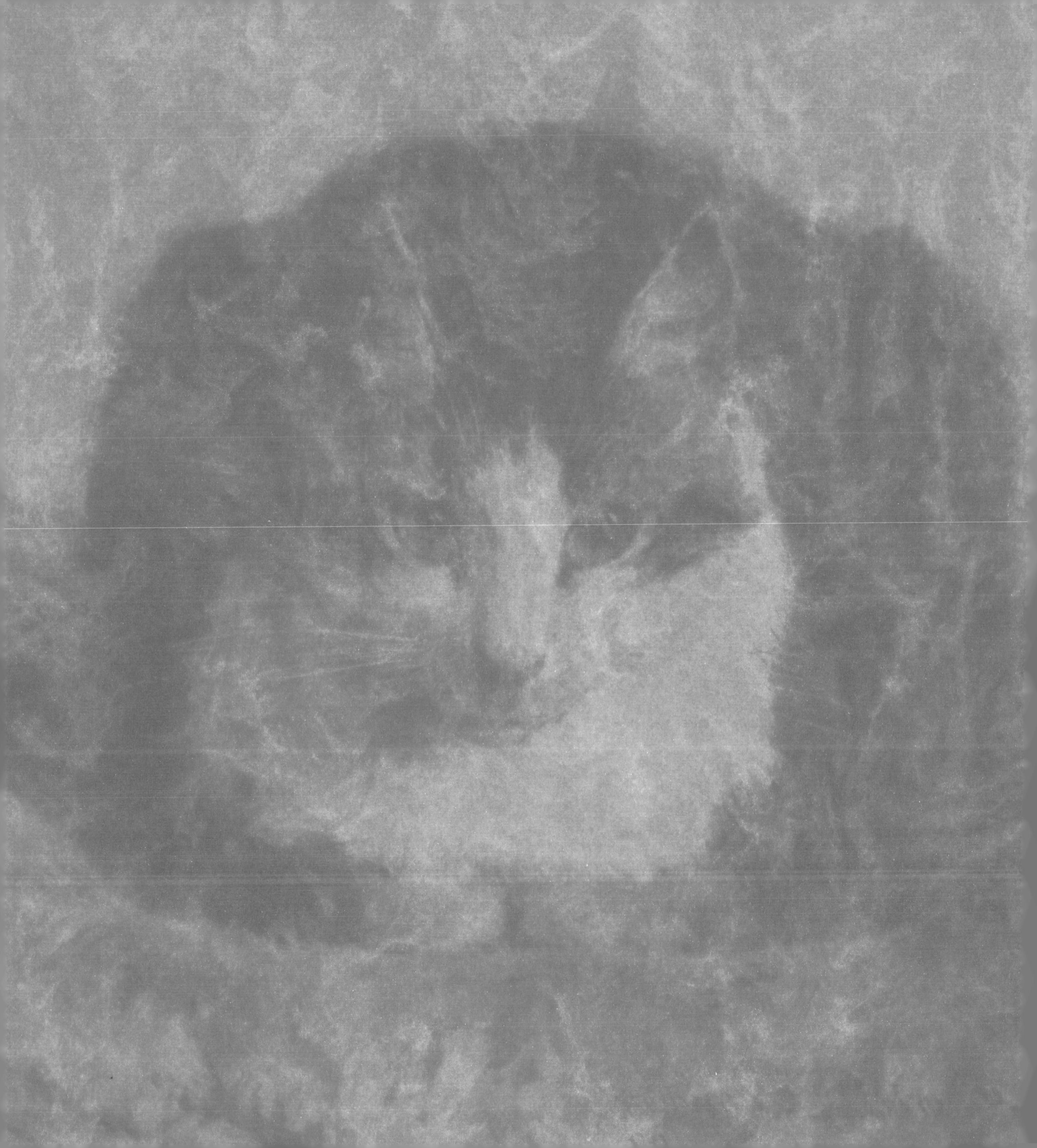

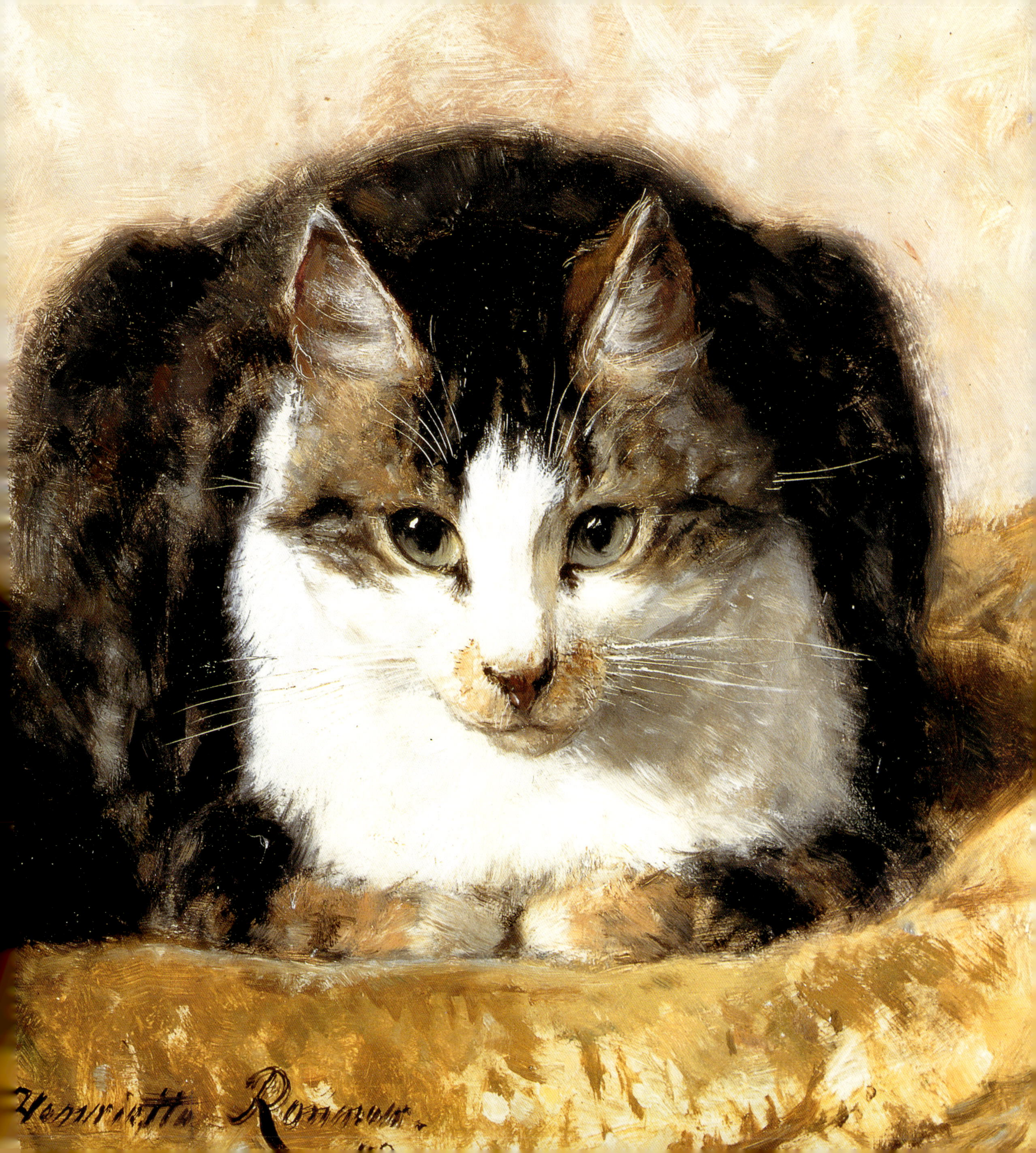

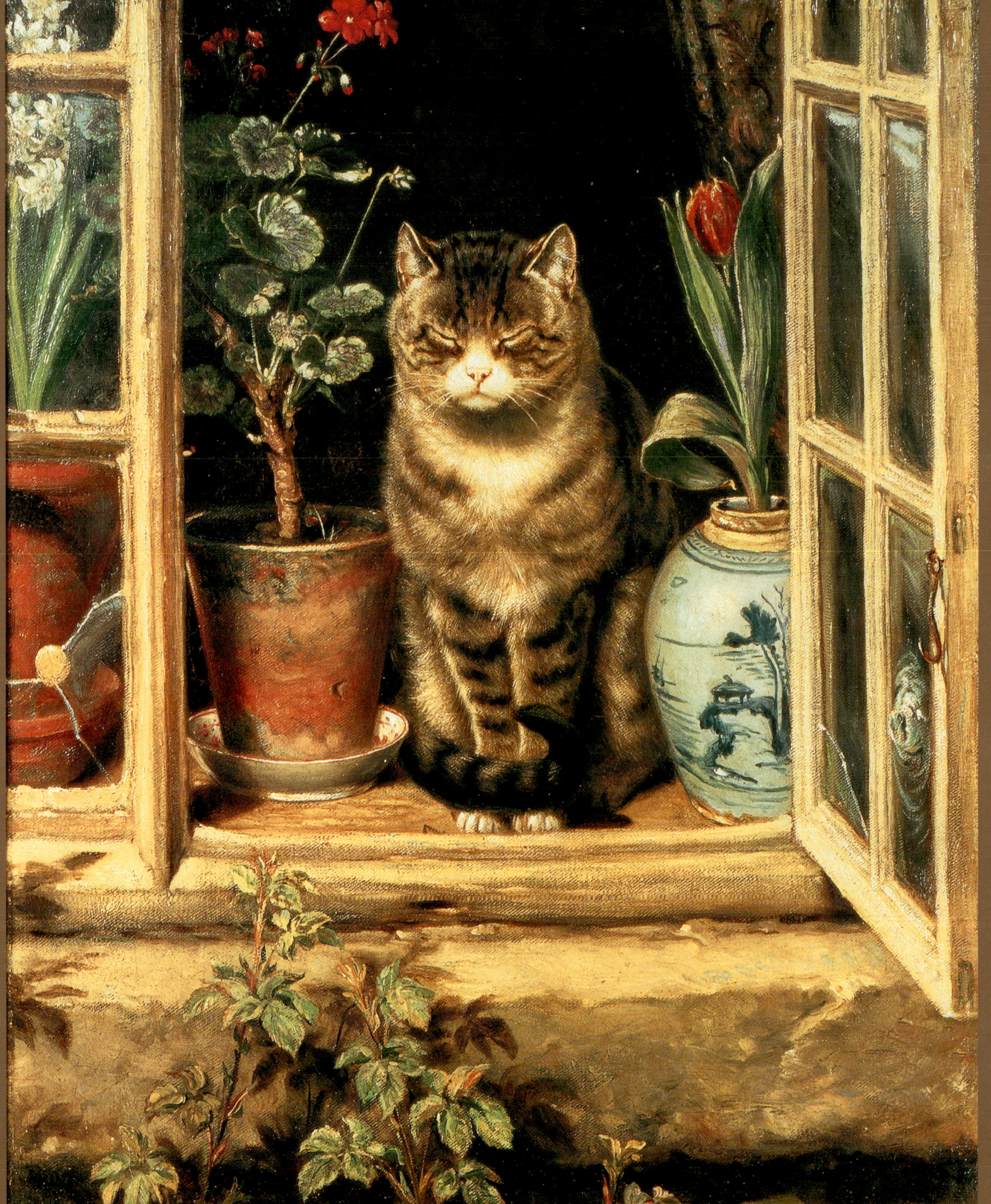

The American writer Mark Twain was a great lover of cats and was greatly impressed by the sleeping habits of a cat he saw in France:

'In the great Zoological Gardens [of Marseilles] we found specimens of all the animals the world produces, I think. . .The boon companion of the colossal elephant was a common cat! This cat had a fashion of climbing up the elephant's hind legs, and roosting on his back. She would sit up there, with her paws curved under her breast, and sleep in the sun half the afternoon. It used to annoy the elephant at first and he would reach up and take her down, but she would go aft and climb up again. She persisted until she finally conquered the elephant's prejudices, and now they are inseparable friends. The cat plays about her comrade's forefeet of his trunk often, until dogs approach, and then she goes aloft out of danger. The elephant has annihilated several dogs laterly, that pressed his companion too closely.'

And, in 1908, Twain wrote a letter about the leisure activities of his cat Tammany and its kittens : 'One of them likes to be crammed into a corner-pocket of the billiard table – which he fits as snugly as does a finger in a glove and then he watches the game (and obstructs it) by the hour, and spoils many a shot by putting out his paw and changing the direction of the ball.'

'Of all God's creatures there is only one that cannot be made the slave of the lash. That one is the cat,' he wrote. 'If man could be crossed with the cat it would improve the man, but it would deteriorate the cat.'

left A Cat in the Window of a Cottage *by Ralph Hedley.*

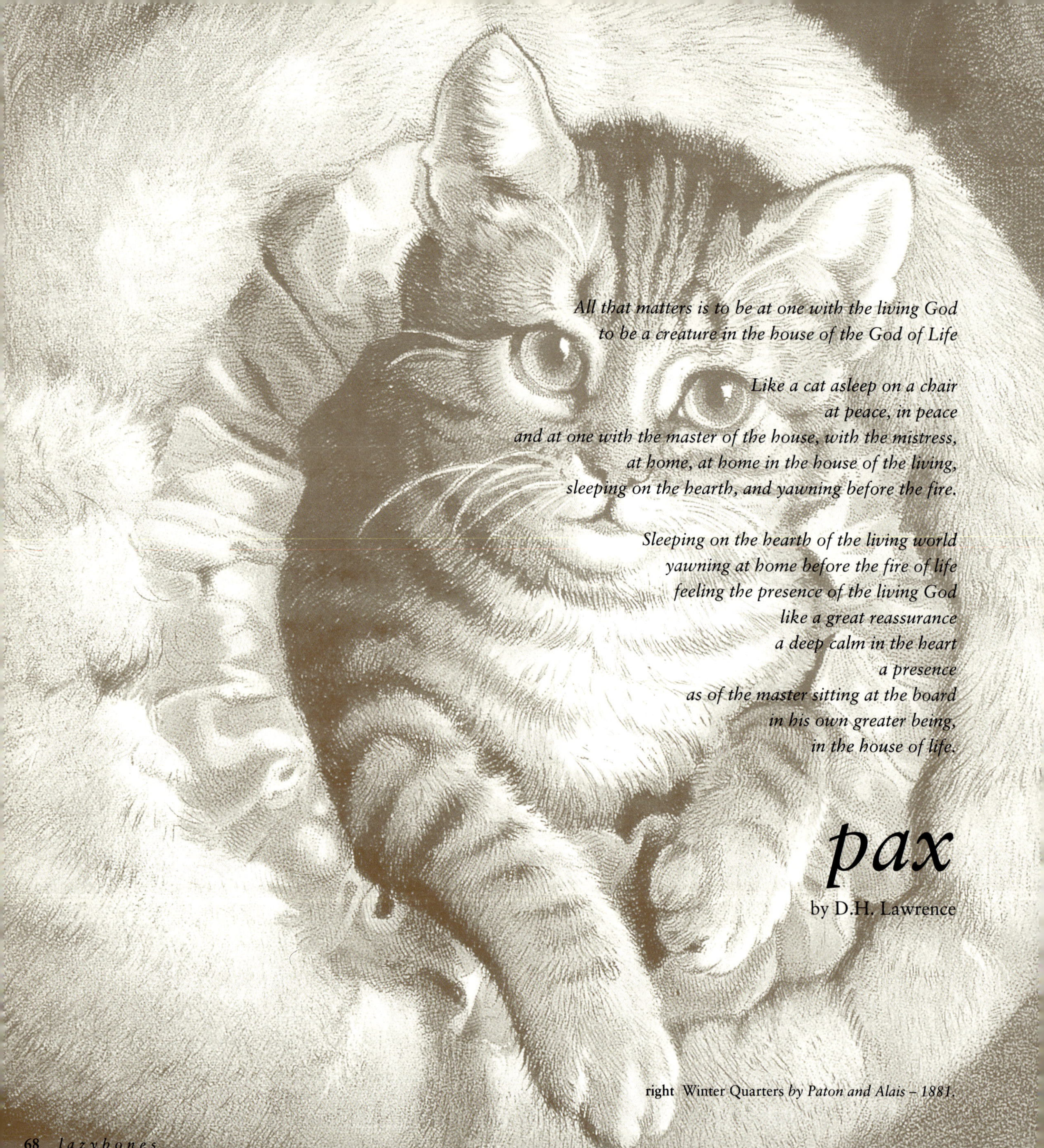

All that matters is to be at one with the living God
to be a creature in the house of the God of Life

Like a cat asleep on a chair
at peace, in peace
and at one with the master of the house, with the mistress,
at home, at home in the house of the living,
sleeping on the hearth, and yawning before the fire.

Sleeping on the hearth of the living world
yawning at home before the fire of life
feeling the presence of the living God
like a great reassurance
a deep calm in the heart
a presence
as of the master sitting at the board
in his own greater being,
in the house of life.

pax

by D.H. Lawrence

right Winter Quarters *by Paton and Alais – 1881.*

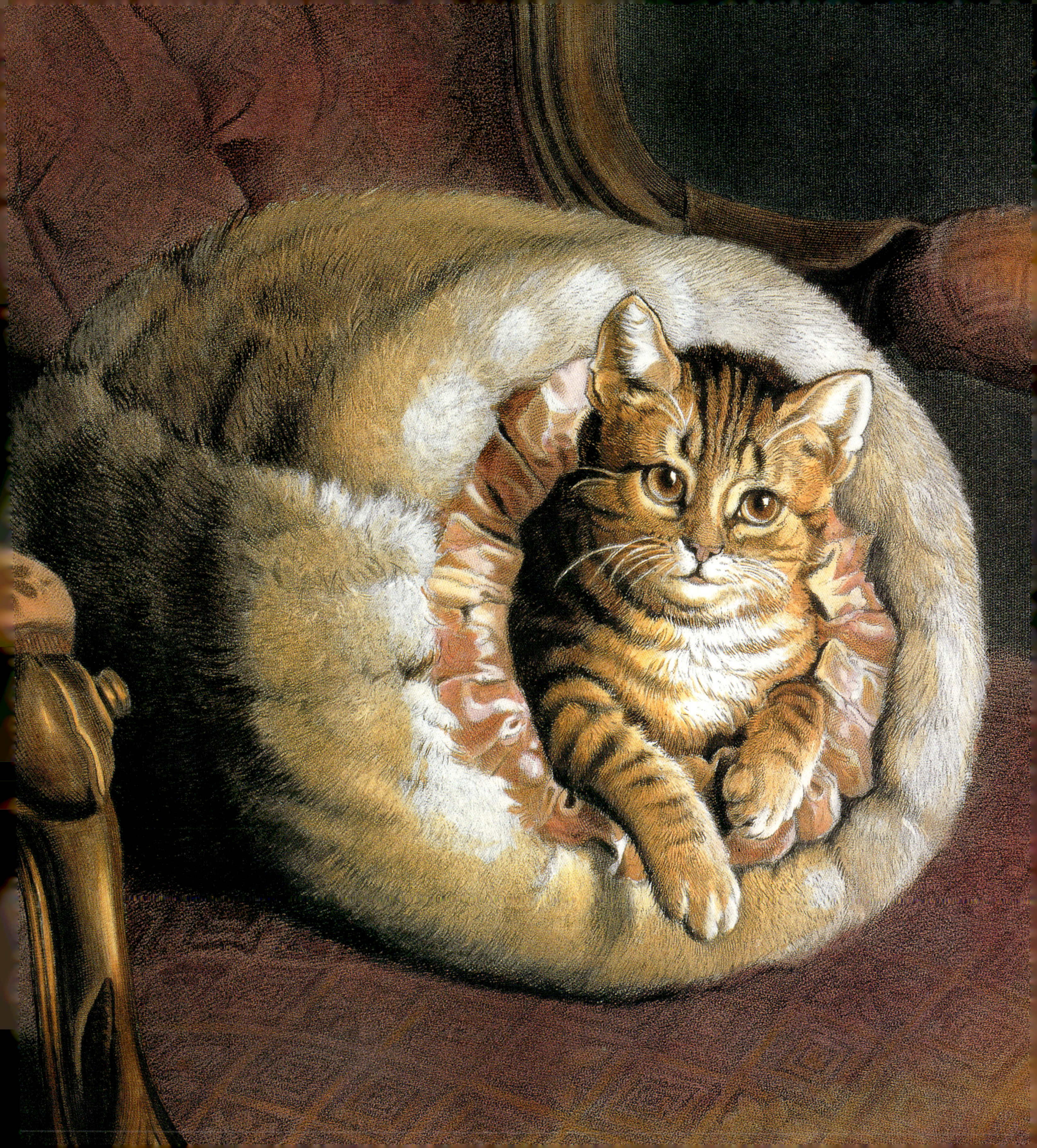

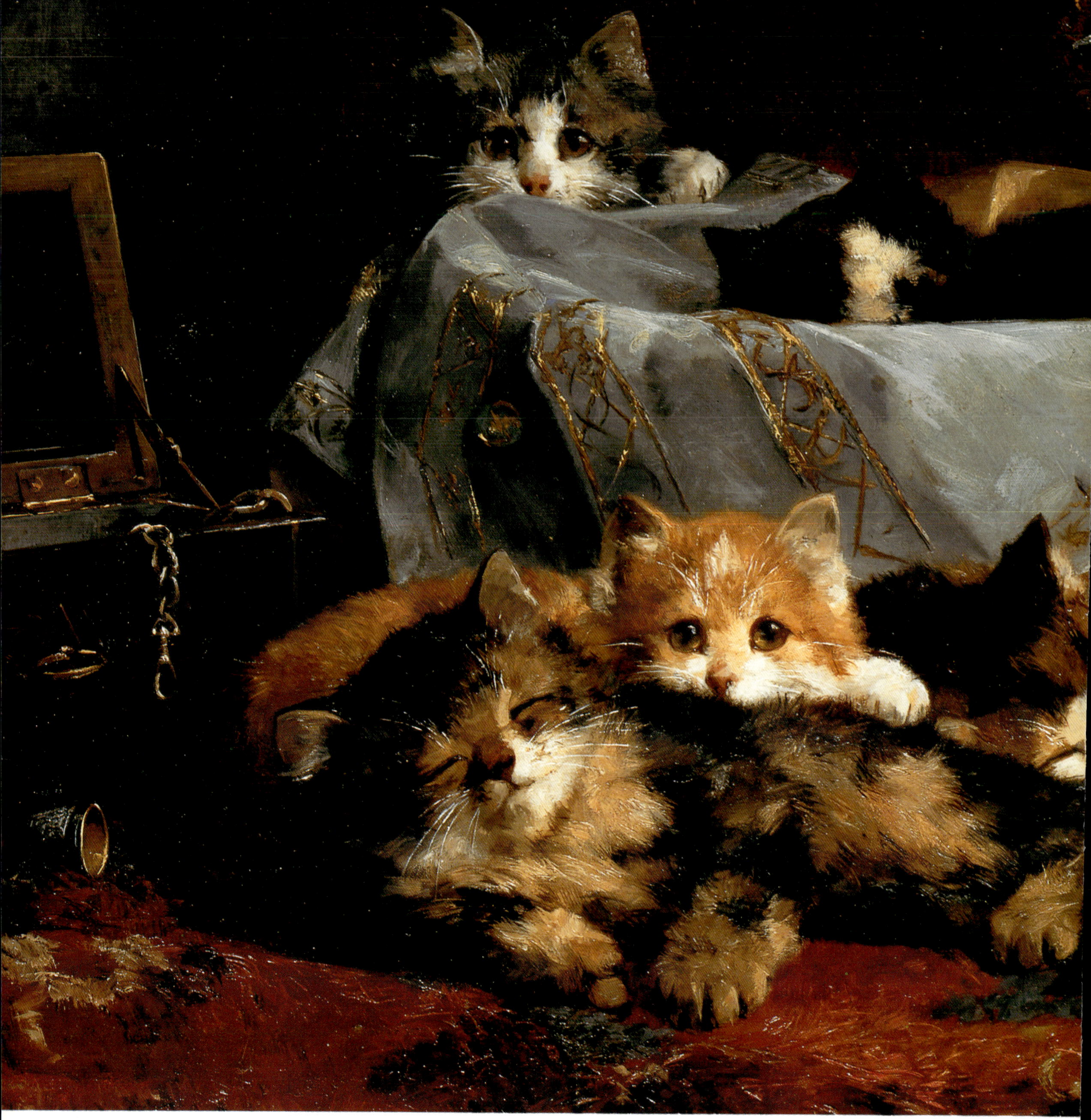

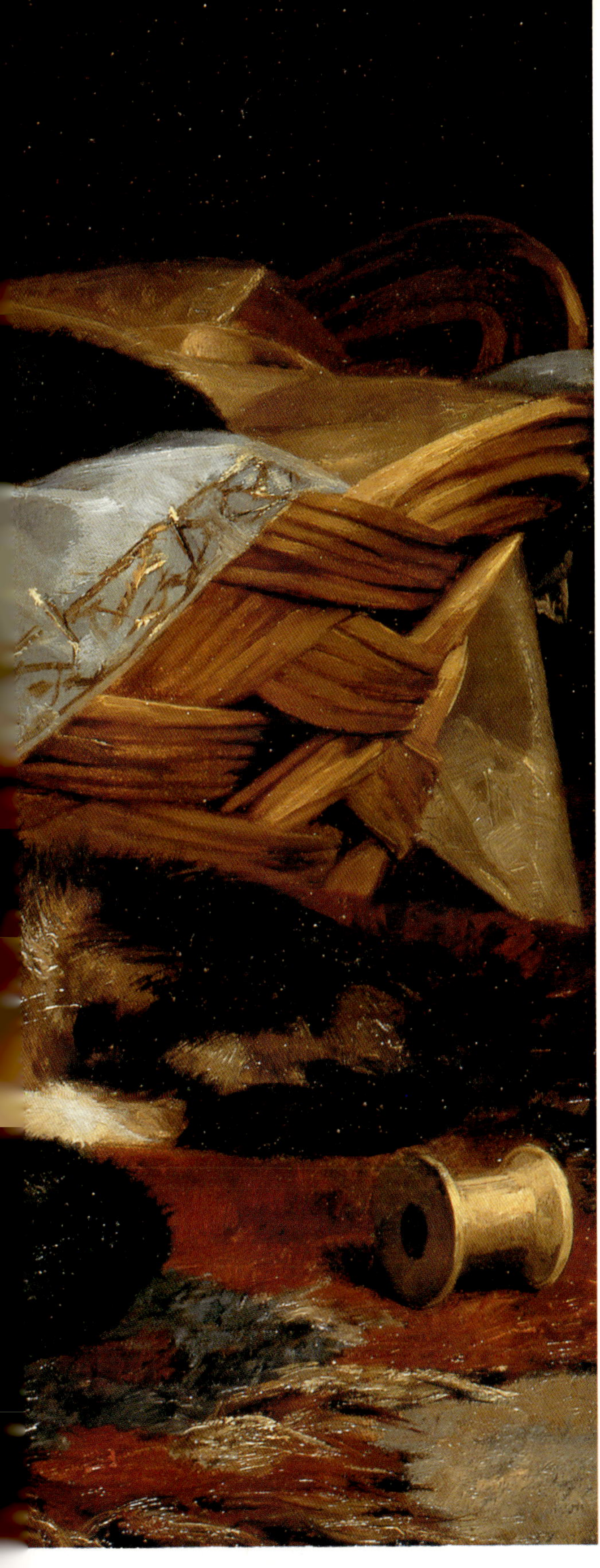

Lord,
I am the cat.
It is not, exactly, that I have something to ask of You!
No –
I ask nothing of anyone –
but,
if You have by some chance, in some celestial barn,
a little white mouse,
or a saucer of milk,
I know someone who would relish them,
Wouldn't You like someday
to put a curse on the whole race of dogs,
If so I should say,
AMEN

the prayer of the cat

Carmen Bernos de Casztold
Translated from the French by Rumer Godden, Faber Prayers from the Ark

left Kittens by a Sewing Basket –
Charles Van Den Eycken

The fervent lover and the sage austere
In their ripe season equally admire
The great soft cats, who, like their masters dear,
Are shivery folk and sit beside the fire.

Friends both of learning and of wantonness,
They hunt where silence and dread shadows are;
Erebus would have yoked their to his car
For funeral coursers had their pride been less.

They take, brooding, the noble attitudes
Of sphinxes stretched in deepest solitudes
That look to slumber in an endless dream:
Their loins are quick with kindlings magical,
And glints of gold, as in a sandy stream,
Vaguely bestar their eyeballs mystical.

cats

Charles Pierce Baudelaire (translated by D.S. MacColl)

left Cat on a Rush Chair *by Koyanagui Sei.*

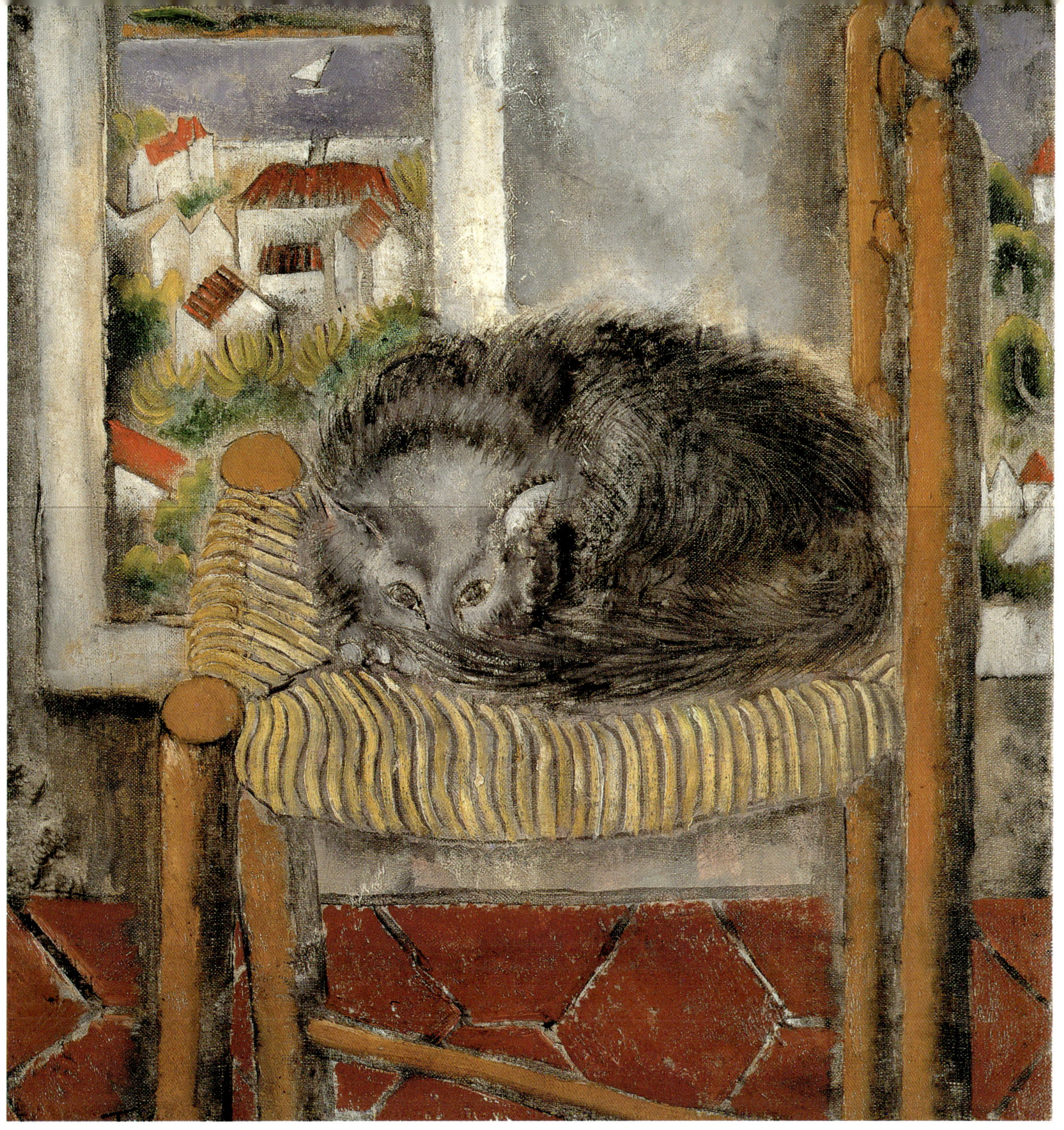

‘It is easy to understand why the rabble dislike cats. A cat is beautiful, it suggests the ideas of luxury, cleanliness, voluptuous pleasure.’

Baudelaire

7

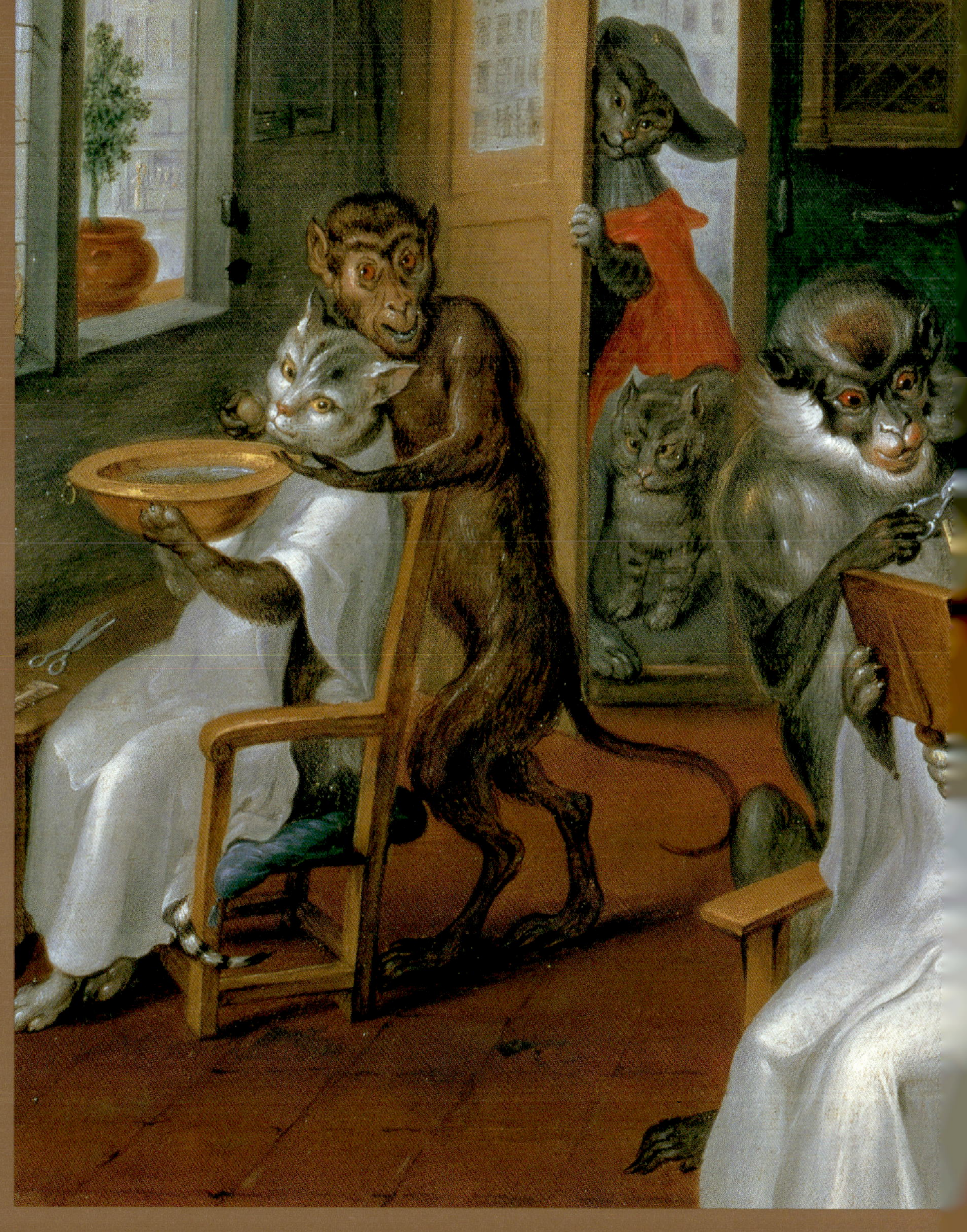

mysterious cats

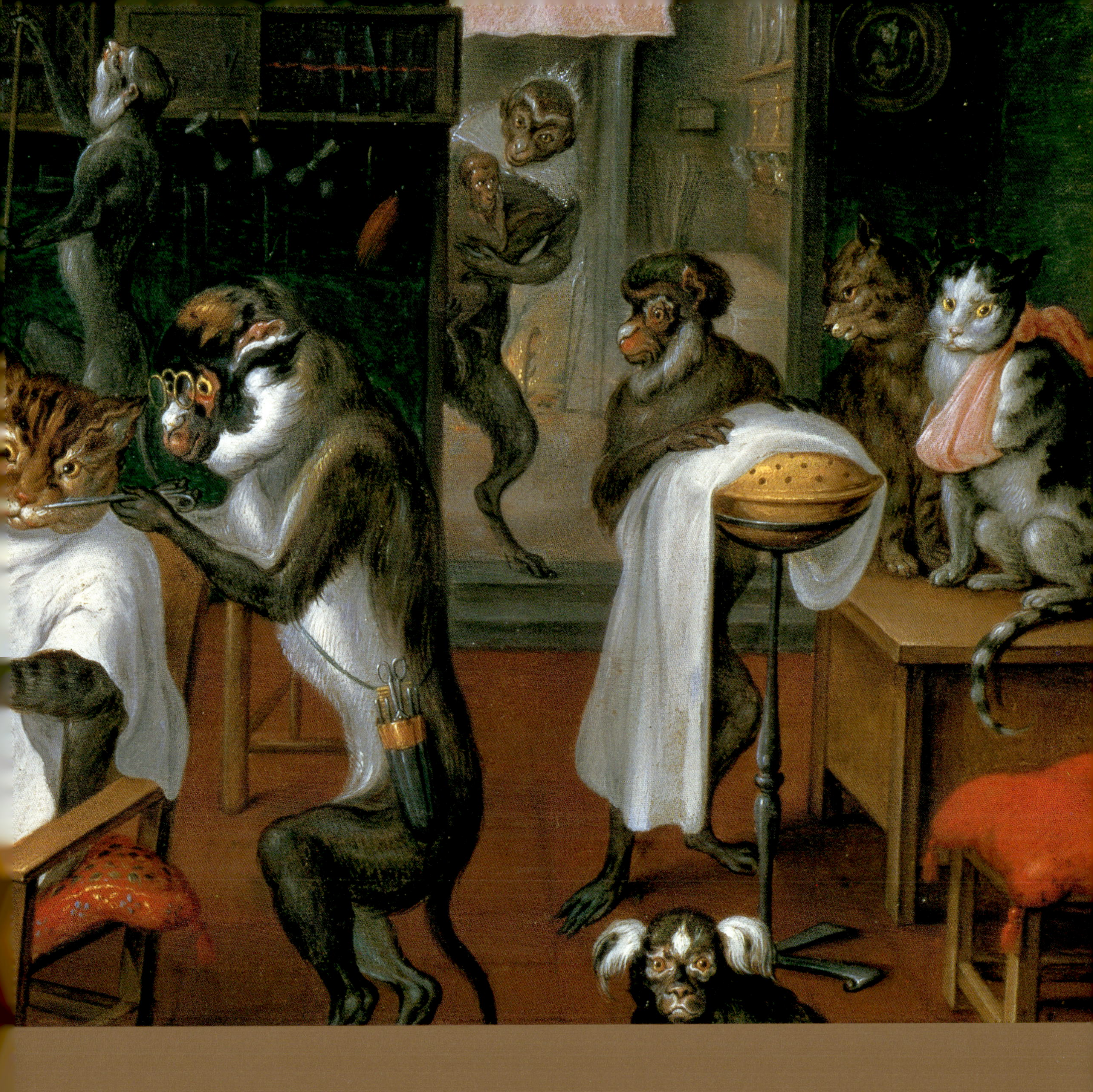

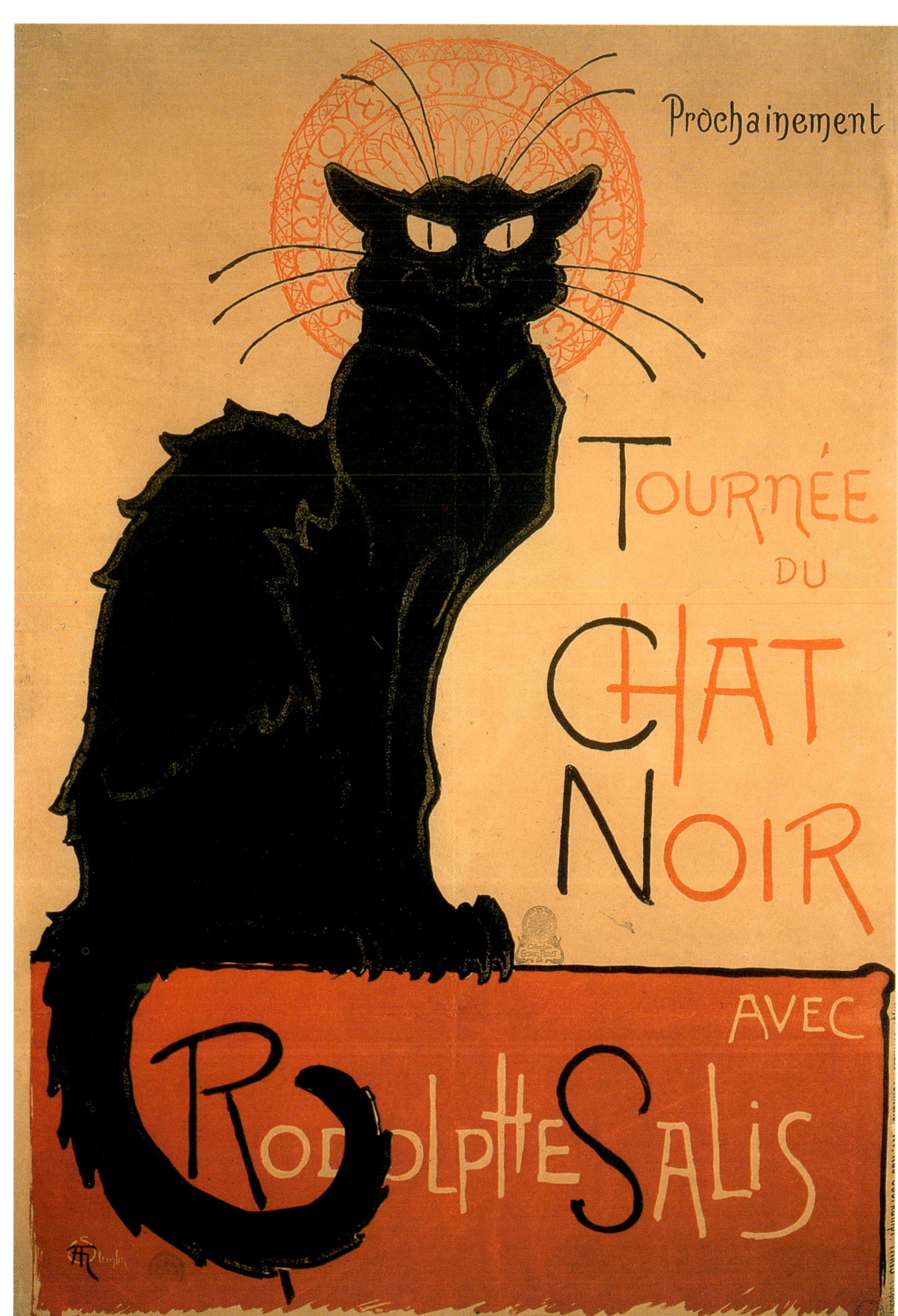
Prochainement
Tournée
du
Chat
Noir
avec
Rodolphe Salis

Cats are supposed to have nine lives. Normally this belief is attributed to the fact that cats are very dexterous and can survives falls from considerable heights. It also has its origins in witchcraft. In the Middle Ages it was thought that, due to an old pact with the devil, a witch could transform herself into a cat nine times. No one knew what would happen if she tried it a tenth time.

Another origin of the belief maybe a folktale told in Germany. Apparently, back in the days when the Black Forest was inhabited by elves and hobgobbins, a poor woodcutter lived in a hovel there. One day, he came home to find a kitten on his doorstep. He was a kind man and took the kitten in to share his meagre supper. But he knew the kitten would have to go because he could scarcely feed himself.

The following day, according to custom, he had to lay out food to propitiate the elves. This meant he had to go without food himself and there was certainly nothing left to feed the kitten with. So he took it out deep into the forest and left it there, in the hope that it would find food by itself. But two days later, the kitten returned.

He took it out into the forest eight more times. Each time it returned, looking bigger and fatter and more healthy. Finally the woodcutter relented and kept the cat. From that day, his luck changed. Jobs started coming his way. Soon he had enough food to feed himself, the cat and the elves. And it was not long before he could afford to move into a snug little cottage in the village. When he was asked about the source of his good fortune he said it was due to his cat's nine lives.

previous page Barber's Shop with Monkeys and Cats, *a 17th Century oil painting by Abraham Teniers.*

left *A poster for the Parisian cabaret Chat Noir, by Steinlen – 1895.*

Cats can also cure diseases as well as inflict them. According to Edward Topsell, in *The History of Four-Footed Beasts:*

'It is reported that the flesh of Cats, salted and sweetened, hath power in it to draw wens from the body and, being warmed, to cure the Hemmorhoids and pains in the veins and back, according to the Verse of Ursinus. In Spain and Gallia Norbon, they eat Cats, but first of all they take away their head and tail, and hang the prepared flesh a night or two in the open cold air, to exhale the savour of it, finding the flesh thereof almost as sweet as a cony. The flesh of Cats can seldom be free from poison, by reason of their daily food, eating Rats and Mice, Wrens and other birds which feed on poison, and above all the brain of the Cat is most venomous, for it being above all measure dry, stoppeth the animal spirits, that they cannot pass into the ventricle, by reason thereof memory faileth, and the infested person falleth into a Phrenzie. The hair of a Cat being eaten unawares, stoppeth the artery and causeth suffocation. To conclude this point it appeareth that this is a dangerous beast, and that therefore as for necessity we are constrained to nourish them for the suppression of vermin: so with a wary eye we must avoid their harms, making more account of their use than of their person.'

right The Love Potion – *1903 – by the Pre-Raphaelite artist Evelyn de Morgan.*

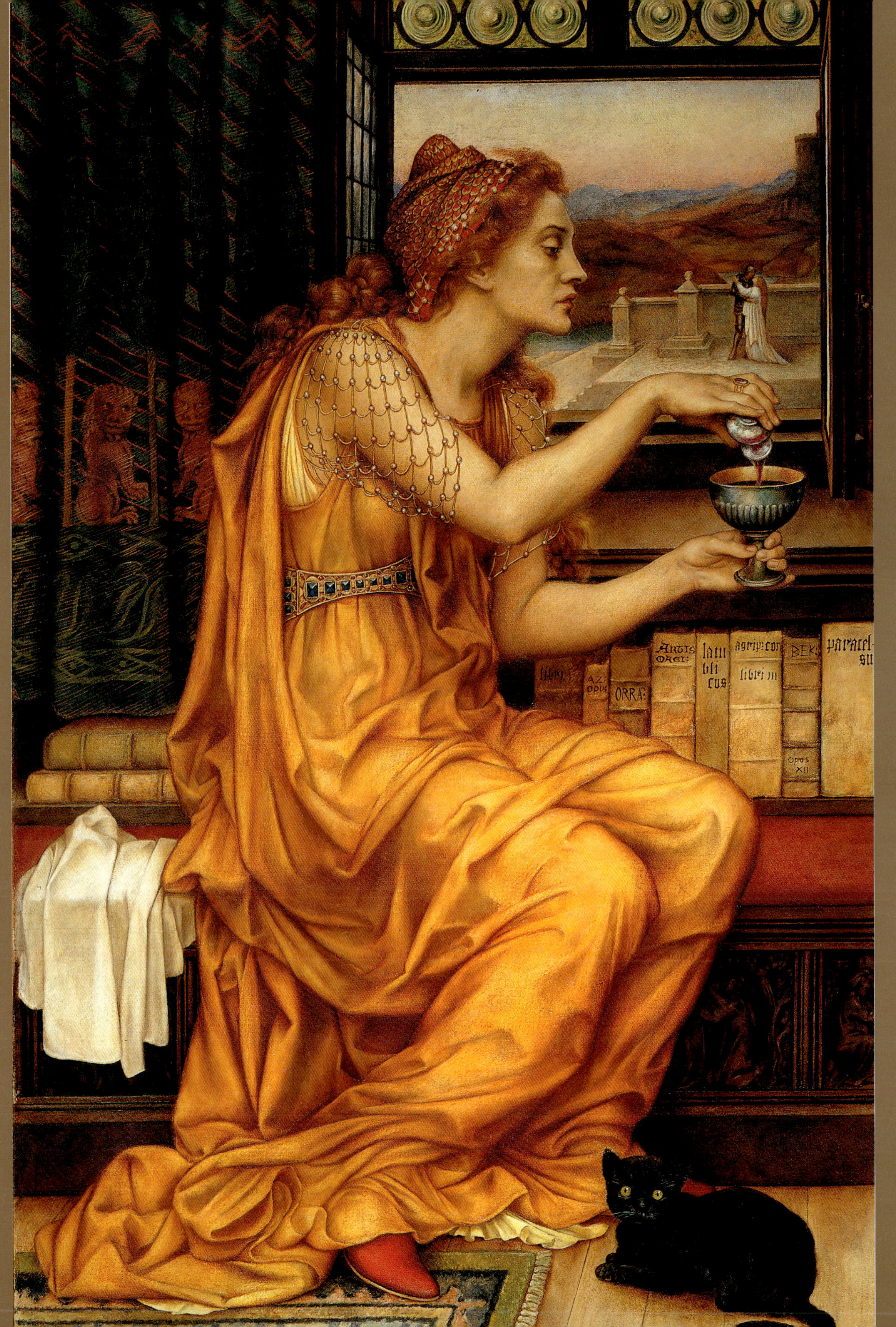
AZ: opus
ORRA:
ARTIS MAGI:
BEK:
opus XII
paracel-su

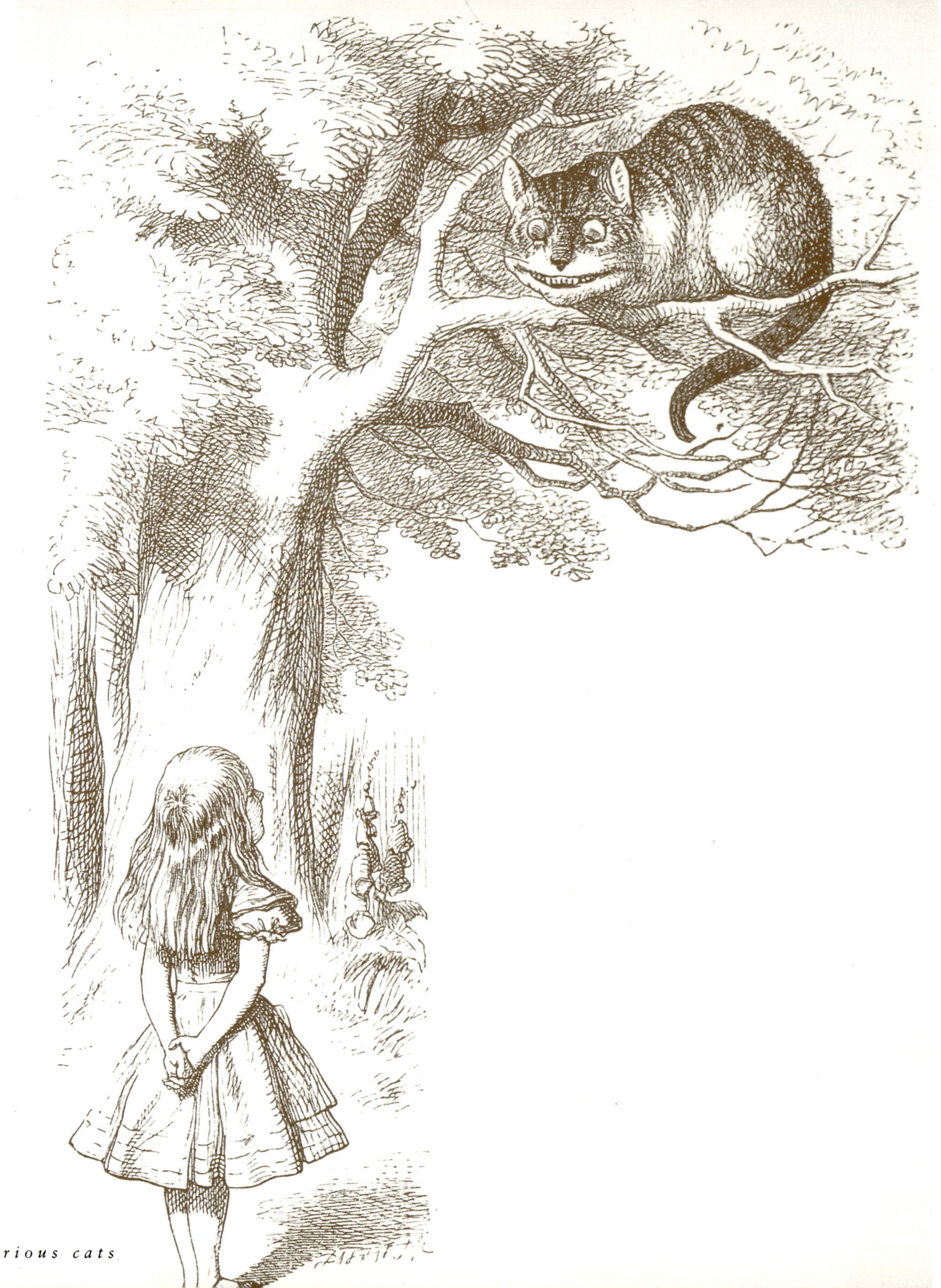

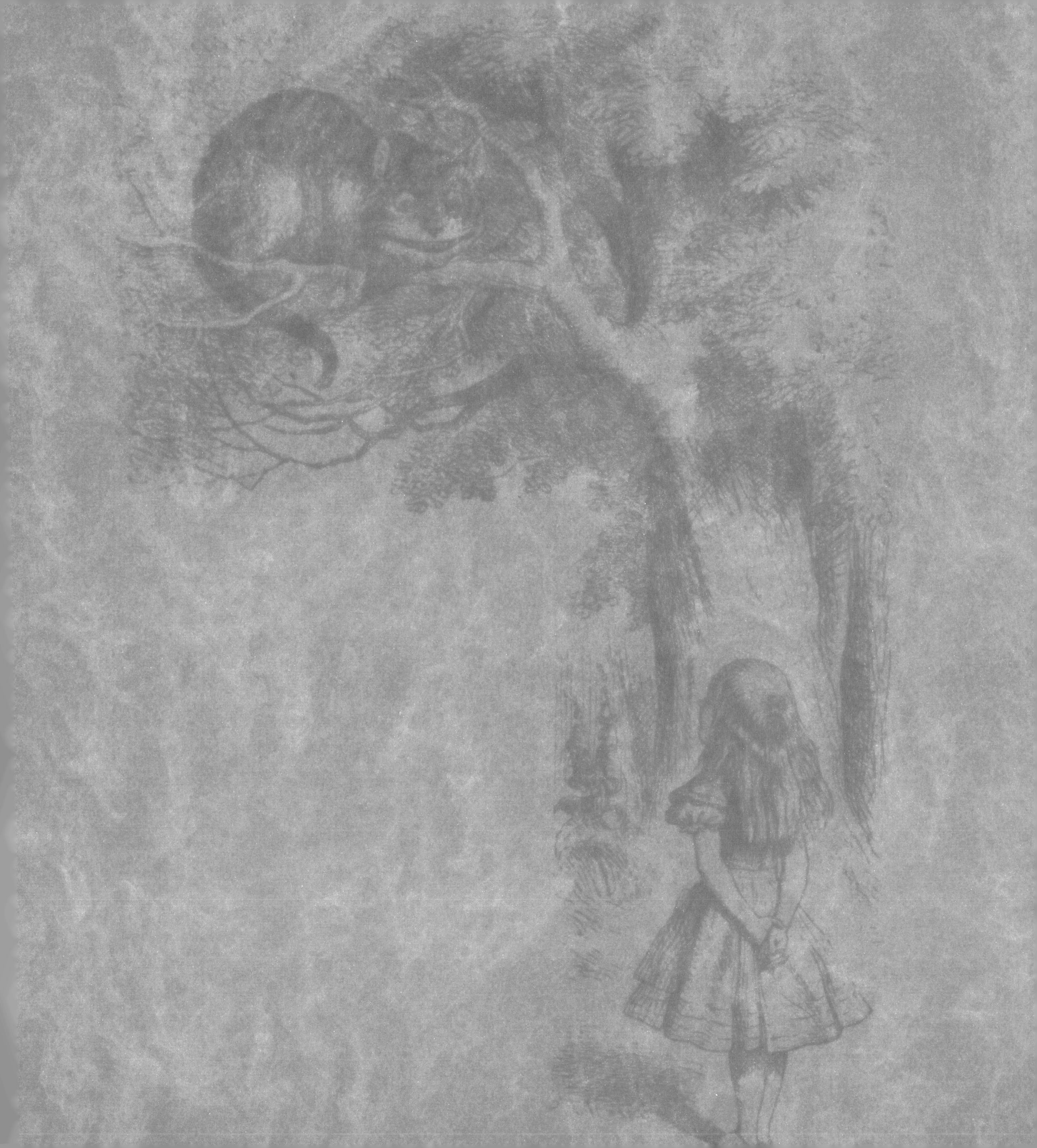

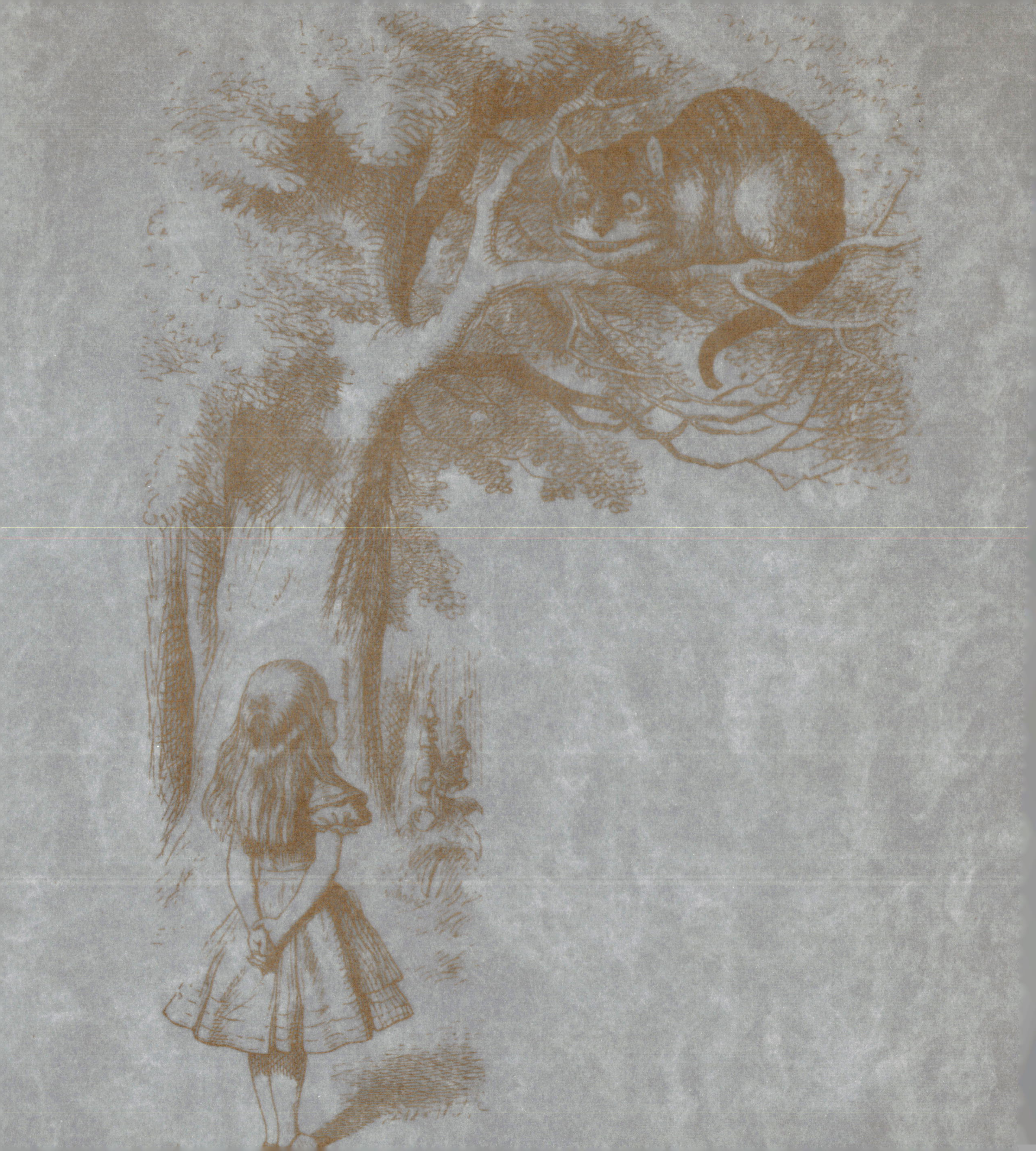

left *Alice meets the Cheshire Cat, illustration by John Tenniel.*

'Do you play croquet with the Queen today?'

'I should like it very much,' said Alice, 'but I haven't been invited yet.'

'You'll see me there,' said the Cat, and vanished.

Alice was not much surprised at this, she was getting so well used to queer things happening. While she was still looking at the place where it had been, it suddenly appeared again.

'Bye-the-bye, what became of the baby?' said the Cat. 'I'd nearly forgotten to ask.'

'It turned into a pig,' Alice answered very quietly, just as if the Cat had come back in a natural way.

'I thought it would,' said the Cat, and vanished again.

Alice waited a little, half-expecting to see it again, but it did not appear and after a minute or two she walked on in the direction in which the March Hare was said to live. 'I've seen hatters before,' she said to herself: 'the Mare will be much the most interest, and perhaps as this is May it won't be raving mad - or at least not so mad as it was in March.' As she said this, she looked up, and there was the Cat again, sitting on the branch of a tree.

'Did you say pig, or fig?' said the Cat.

'I said pig,' replied Alice; 'and I wish you wouldn't keep appearing and vanishing so suddenly: you make one quite giddy.'

'All right,' said the Cat; and this time it vanished quite slowly, beginning with the end of it's tail, and ending with the grin, which remained some time after the rest had gone. 'Well! I've often seen a cat without a grin,' thought Alice; 'but a grin without a cat! It's the most curious thing I ever saw in all my life!'

Lewis Carroll, *Alice in Wonderland*

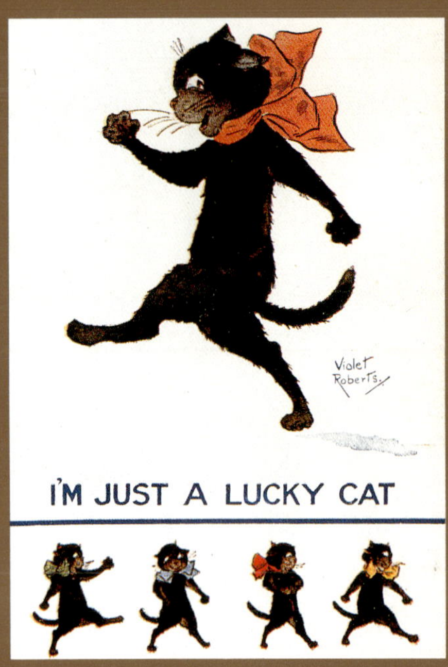

Burning cats to celebrate Lent had begun in Metz, in 962, where hundreds were incinerated. It was Pope Gregory IX that proclaimed the link between black cats and the devil. In the 15th Century, Pope Innocent VIII began the persecution of those who worshipped cats. In France, on the eve of St John, a feast was held. Bonfires were lit and local cats hurled into it. Their owners, largely old women, were tried for witchcraft and condemned to death along with their cats. This practice continued for nearly two hundred years.

At early witch trials, many women admitted to taking nocturnal flights led by a lady called Frejya or Holda. She would be surrounded by cats or travel on a chariot pulled by cats. In Scandinavian countries, four bowls of milk were left outside the door at night for Frejya's cats.

above Lucky Black Cat *by Violet Roberts.*
right The Witch, *colour lithography by Hans Thoma, 1870.*

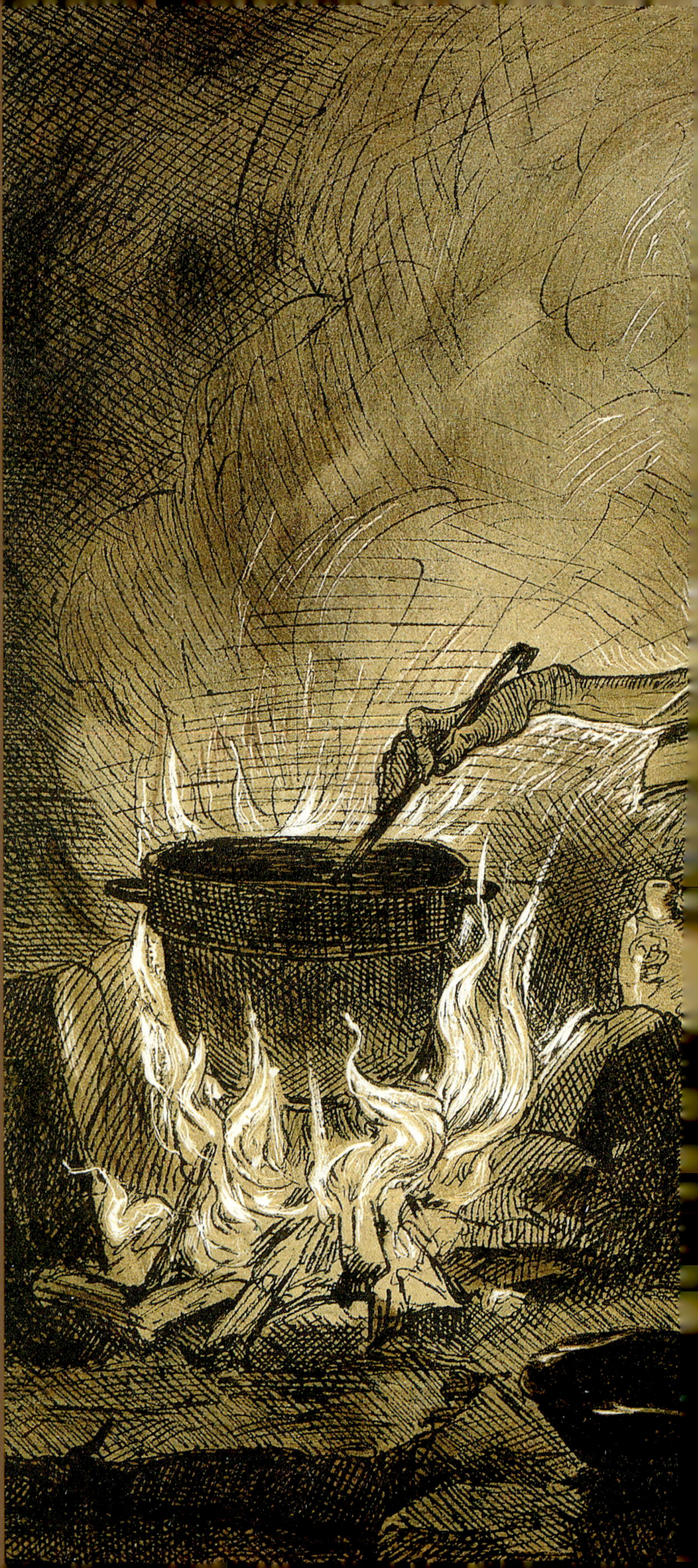

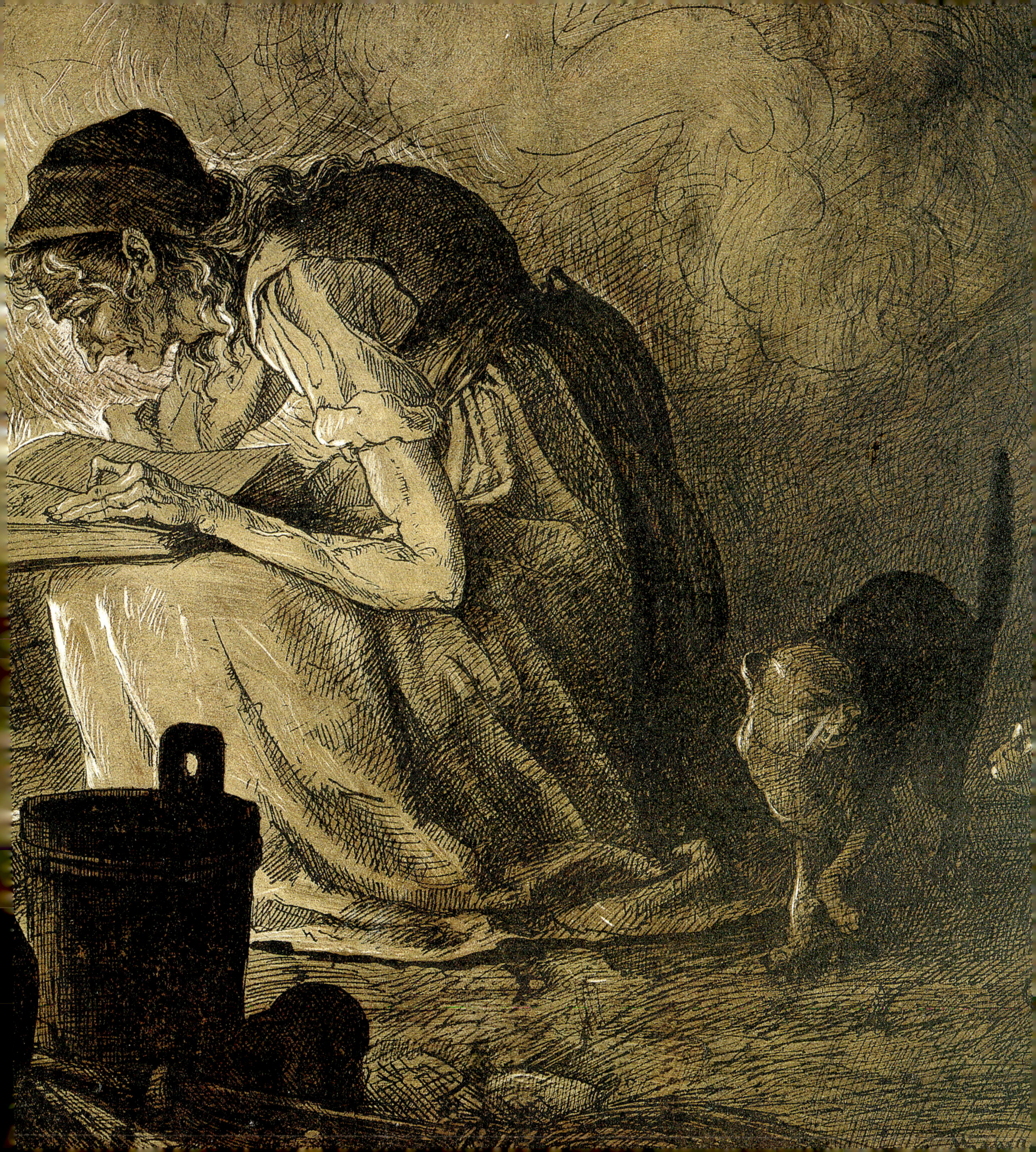

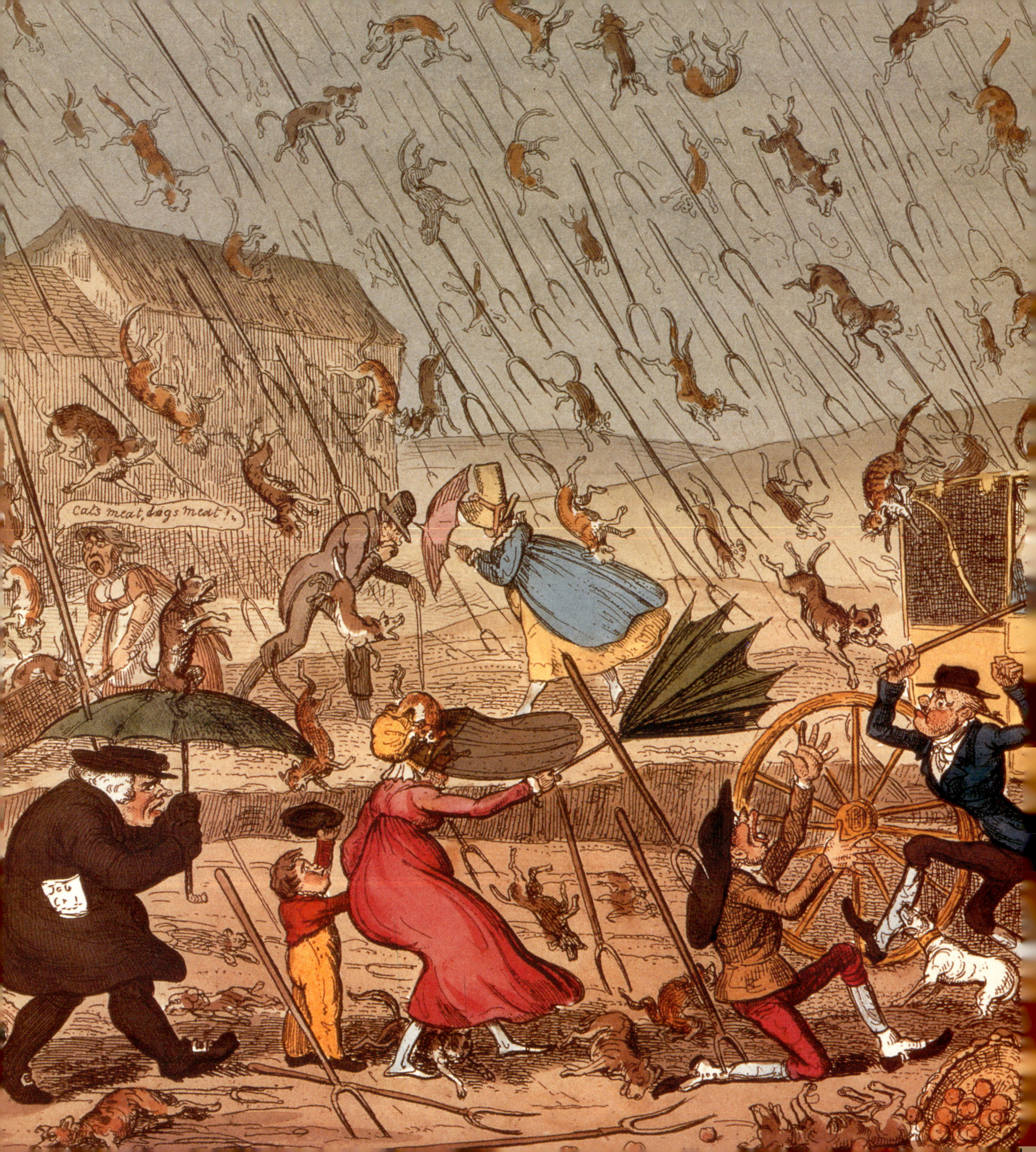
Cats meat, dogs meat!

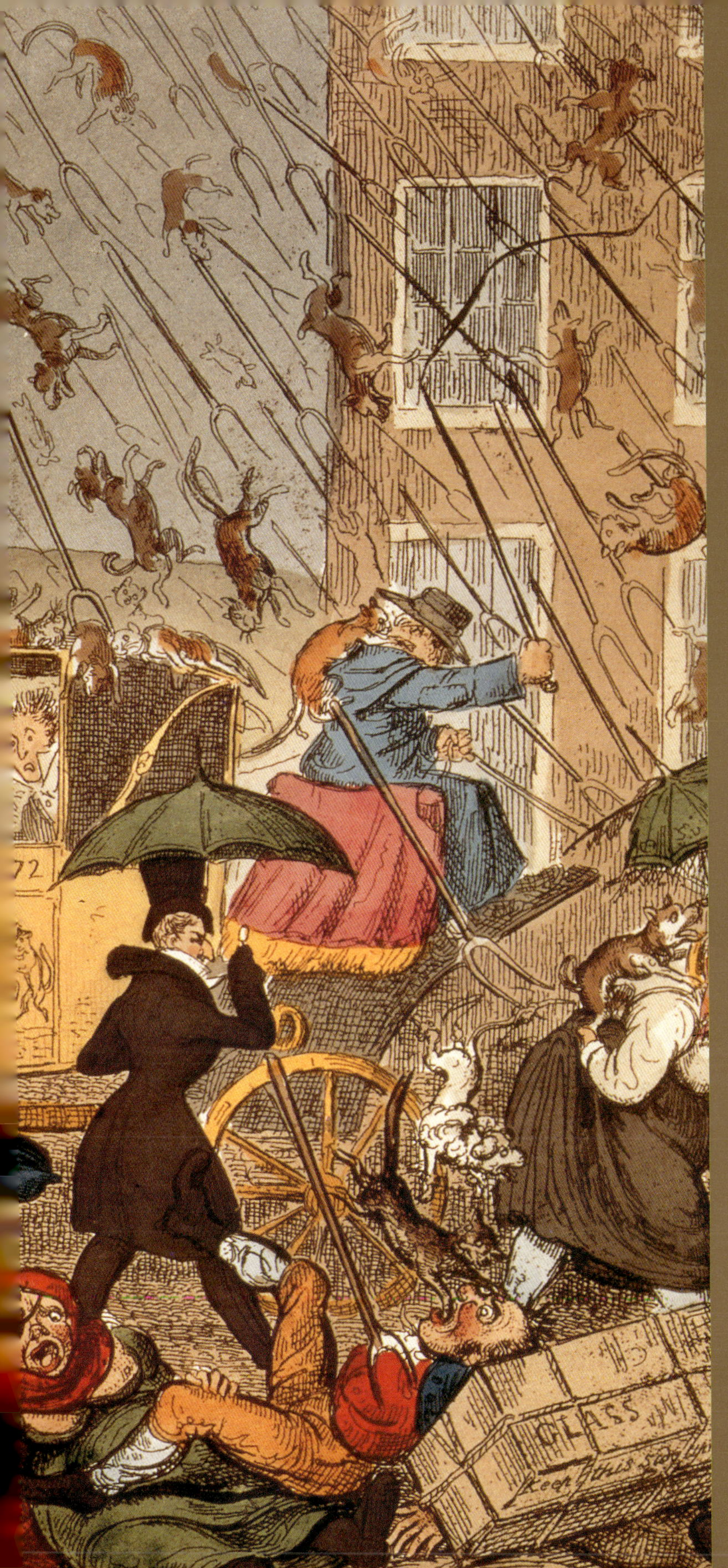

8

literary cats

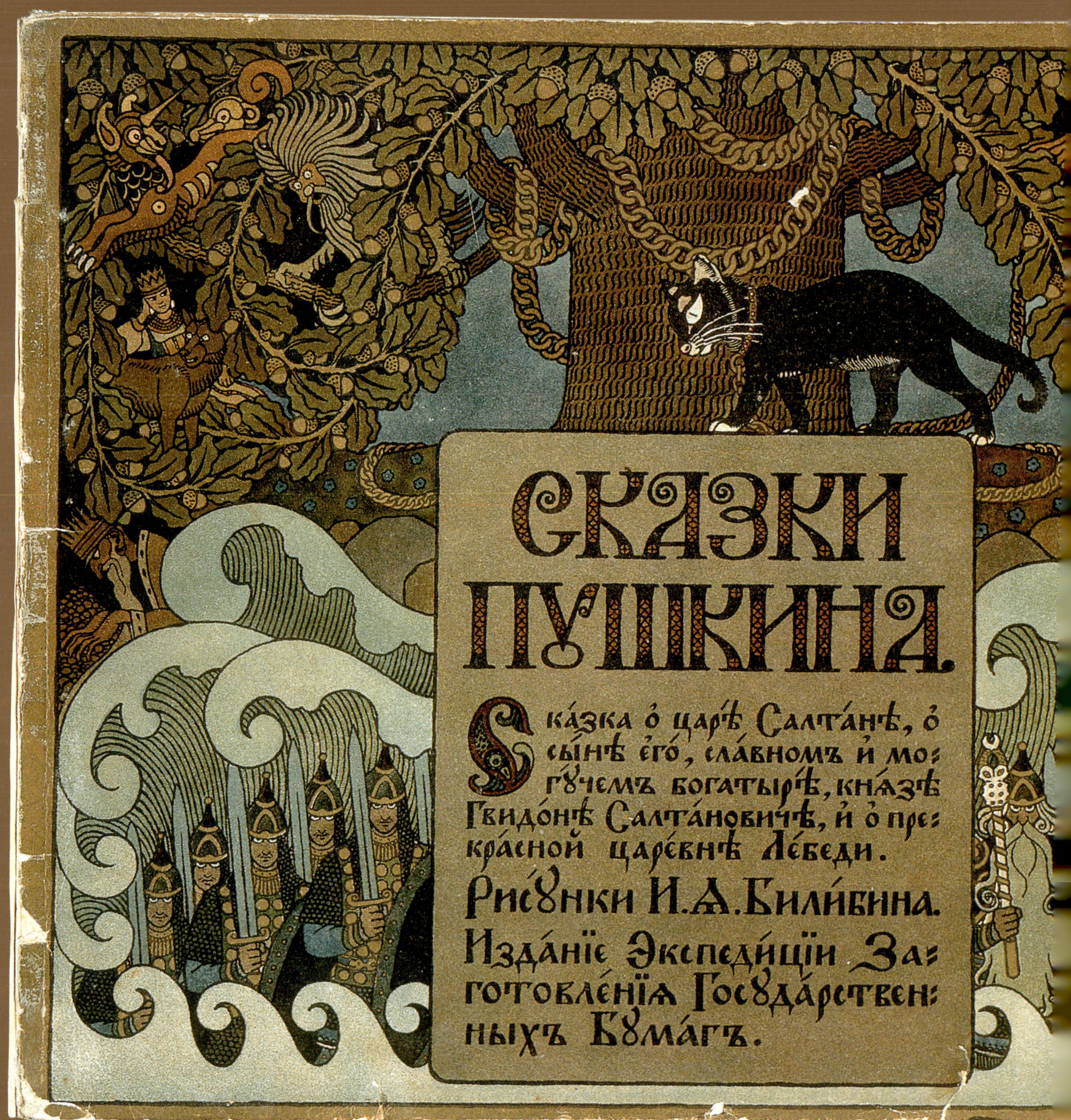

Сказки Пушкина.
Сказка о царѣ Салтанѣ, о сынѣ его, славномъ и могучемъ богатырѣ, князѣ Гвидонѣ Салтановичѣ, и о прекрасной царевнѣ Лебеди.
Рисунки И. Я. Билибина.
Изданіе Экспедиціи Заготовленія Государственныхъ Бумагъ.

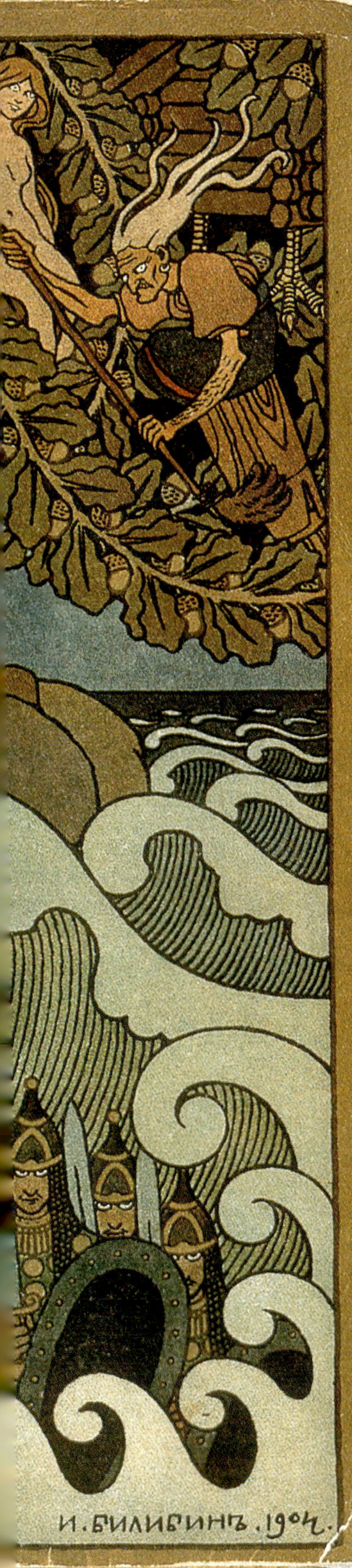

previous page Raining Cats, Dogs and Pitchforks, *by George Cruikshank – 1820.*

left The Tale of Tsar Sultan *by Russian poet Alexander Pushkin – with illustrations by Ivan Jakovlevich, 1832.*

Cat! who hast pass'd thy grand climacteric,
How many mice and rats hast in thy days
Destroy'd? How many tit bits stolen? Gaze
With those bright languid segments green, and prick
Those velvet ears – but pr'ythee do not stick
Thy latent talons in me – and upraise
Thy gentle mew – and tell me all thy frays,
Of fish and mice, and rats and tender chick.
Nay, look not down, nor lick thy dainty wrists –
For all thy wheezy asthma – and for all
Thy tail's tip is nick'd off – and though the fists
Of many a maid have given thee many a maul,
Still is that fur as soft, as when the lists
In youth thou enter'dest on glass bottled wall.

to mrs reynolds' cat

John Keats.

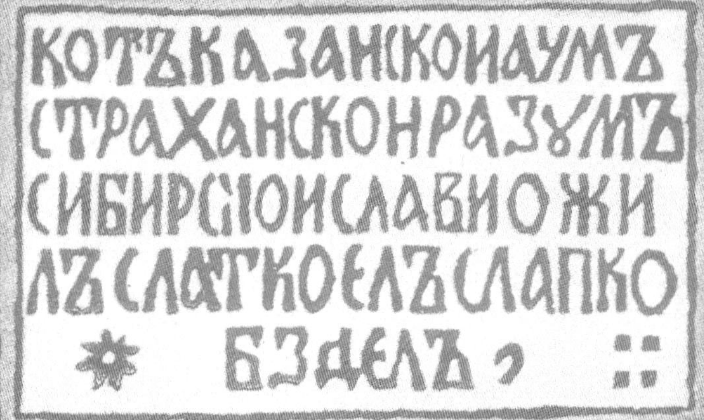

Stately, kindly, lordly friend,
Condescend
Here to sit by me, and turn
Glorious eyes that smile and burn,
Golden eyes, love's lustrous meed,
On the golden page I read.

All your wondrous wealth of hair,
Dark and fair,
Silken-shaggy, soft and bright
As the clouds and beams of night,
Pays my reverent hand's caress
Back with friendlier gentleness.

Dogs may fawn on all and some
As they come;
You, a friend of loftier mind,
Answer friends alone in kind.
Just your foot upon my hand
Softly bids it understand...

What within you wakes with day
Who can say?
All too little may we tell,
Friends who like each other well,
What might haply, if me might,
Bid us read our lives aright.

to a cat

Algernon Charles Swinburne

right *Illustration from a famous Russian fairystory* – The Tomcat of Kasan.

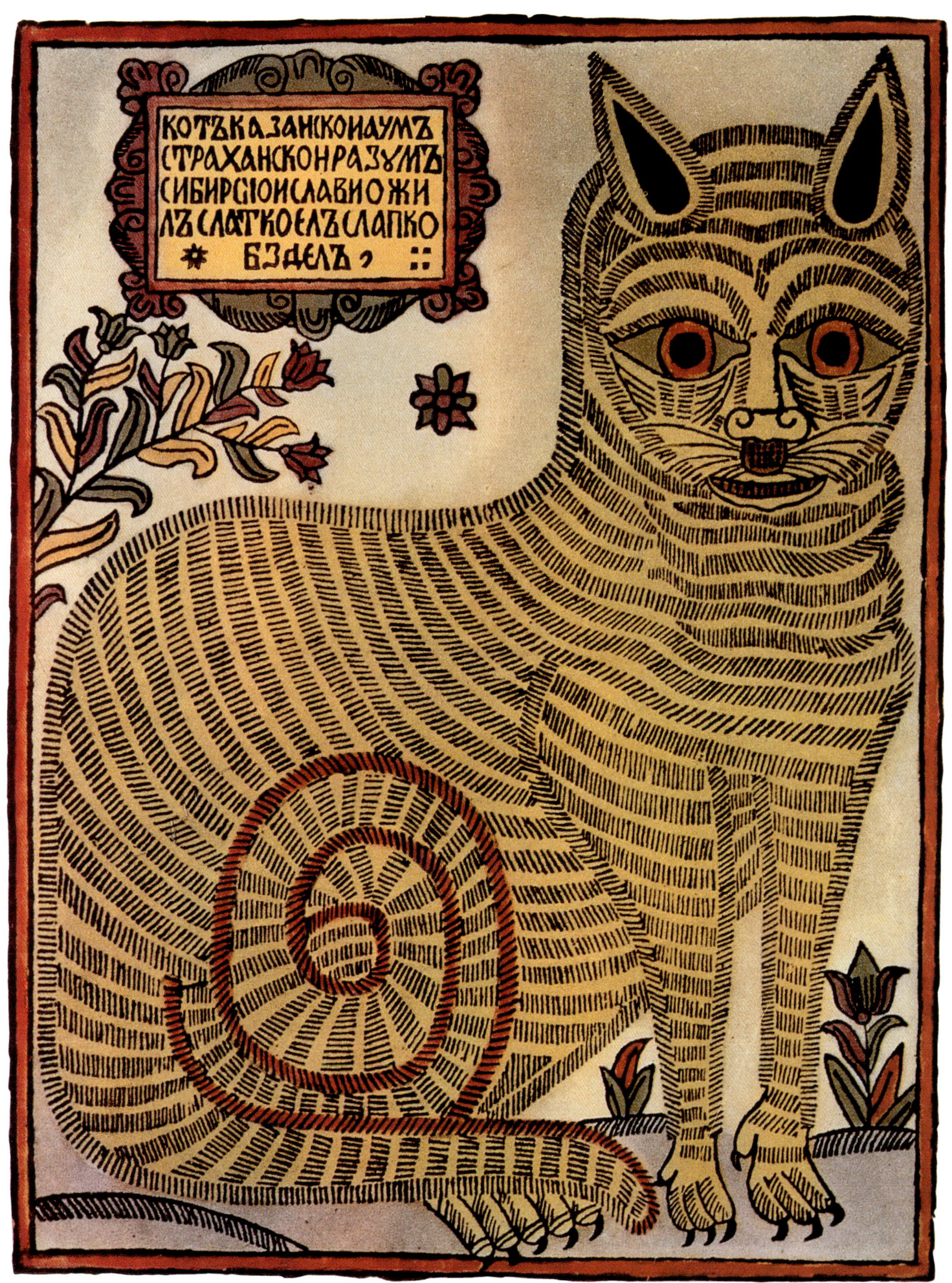

КОТЪКАЗАНСКОИАУМЪ
СТРАХАНСКОИРАЗУМЪ
СИБИРСКОИСЛАВИОЖИ
ЛЪСЛАТКОЕЛЪСЛАПКО
БЗДЕЛЪ

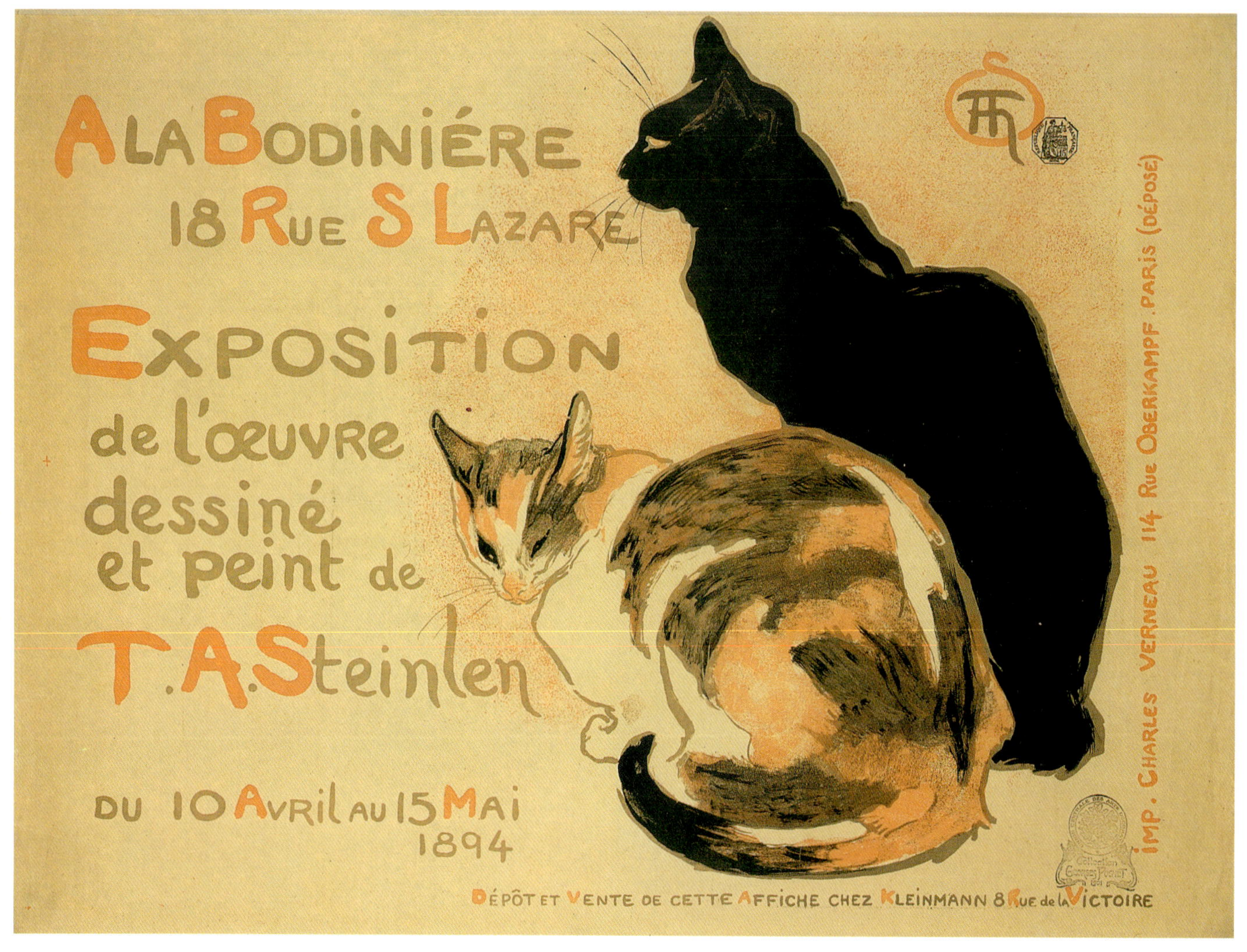

Edgar Allan Poe wrote a horror story called *The Black Cat*. In a drunken rage, an alcoholic tortured his cat Pluto, then hanged it. Drinking more than ever through guilt, the man sought out a replacement.

'One night as I sat, half stupefied in a den of more than infamy, my attention was suddenly drawn to some black object reposing upon the head of one of the immense hogsheads of gin, or of rum, which constituted the chief furniture of the apartment. I had been looking steadily at the top of this hogshead for some minutes, and what now caused me surprise was the fact that I had not sooner perceived the object thereon. I approached it, and touched it with my hand. I was a black cat – a very large one – fully as large as Pluto, and closely resembling him in very respect but one. Pluto had not a white hair upon any portion of his body; but this cat had a large, although indefinite, blotch of white, covering nearly the whole region of the breast.

Upon my touching him, he immediately arose, purred loudly, rubbed against my hand, and appeared delighted with my notice. This, then, was the very creature of which I was in search. I at once offered to purchase it of the landlord; but this person made no claim to it – knew nothing of it – had never seen it before.

I continued my caresses; and when I prepared to go home, the animal evinced a disposition to accompany me. I permitted it to do so, occasionally stooping and patting it as I proceeded. When it reached the house it domesticated itself at once, and became immediately a great favourite with my wife.

For my own part, I soon found a dislike to it arising in me. This was just the reverse of what I had anticipated; but – I know not how or why it was – its evident fondness for myself rather disgusted and annoyed. By slow degrees these feelings of disgust and annoyance rose into the bitterness of hatred. I avoided the creature; a certain sense of shame, and the remembrance of my former deed of cruelty, prevented me from physically abusing it. I did not for some weeks strike it or otherwise violently ill-use it; but gradually – very gradually – I came to look upon it with unutterable loathing, and to flee silently from its odious presence, as from the breath of pestilence.'

Eventually, he tried to kill this cat too. His wife tried to stop him and, by accident, he killed her instead. He walled up her body in the cellar. When the police came to search the house, the cat's cries lead them to the corpse. He had, accidentally, bricked the cat up in his wife's makeshift tomb.

left *A poster by Steinlen, 1894.*
right Cat – *Roger Hilton, 1974.*

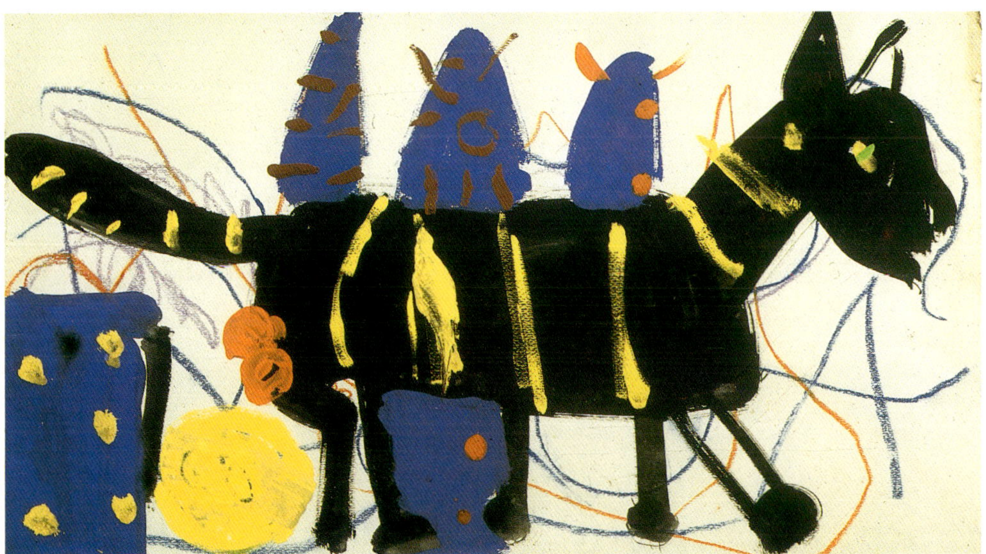

The most famous image of Puss in Boots was created by the French artist Gustave Dore (1832-1883). One of the most important illustrators of the 19th Century, he made dramatic and imaginative engravings for more than 120 books. These included Milton's *Paradise Lost,* Dante's *Divine Comedy* and Balzac's *Droll Stories*. He also worked on a number of collections of folk stories, including Las Fontaine's *Fables* and Charles Perrault's *Histoires ou contes du temps passe*. Published in 1697, Perrault's classic tome gives eight traditional fairy tales their classic form. Among them are *Bluebeard, Sleeping Beauty* and *Puss in Boots*. Dore was hired to illustrate the 1862 edition. For it, he produced the behatted, cloaked and thigh-booted Puss that has been copied ever since.

right *A French postcard depicting Puss In Boots*
below Puss In Boots, *a blockprint from 1912 of the famous tale.*

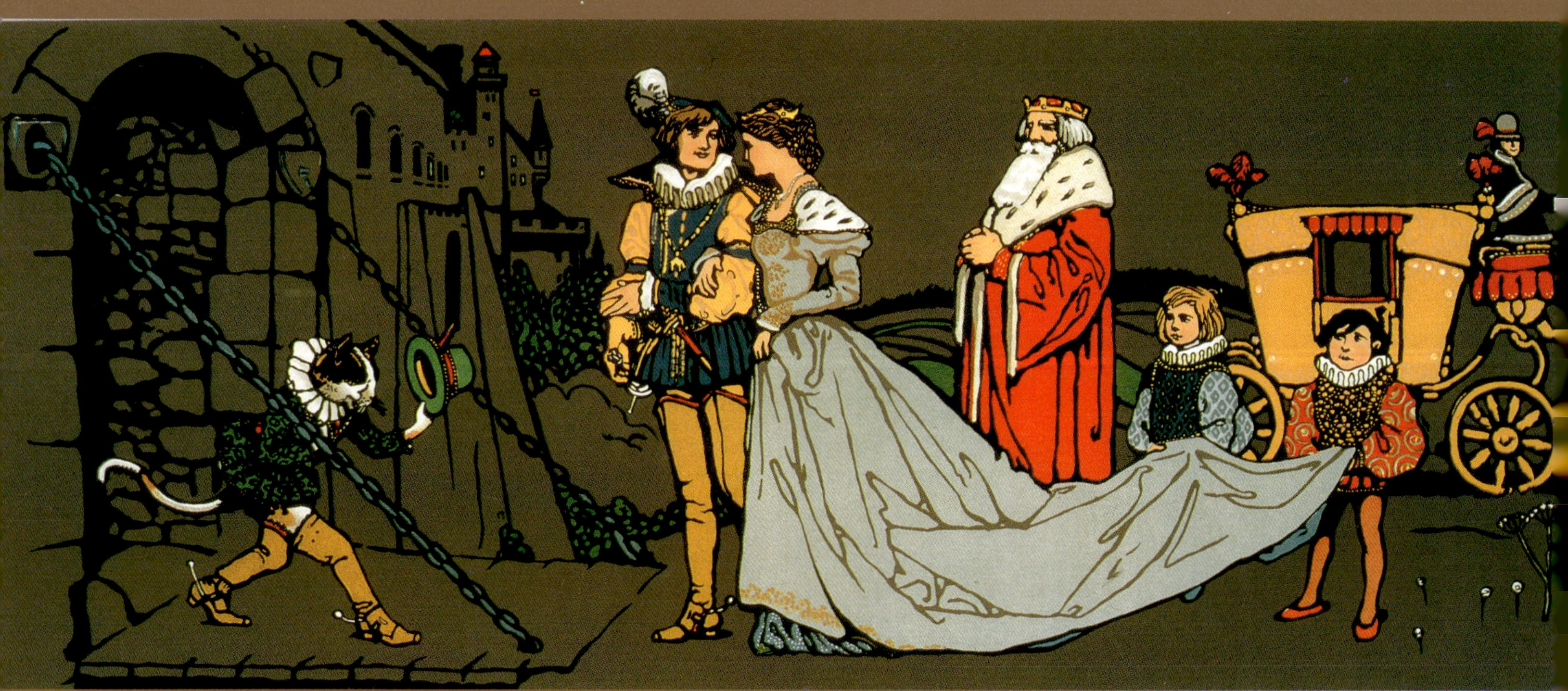

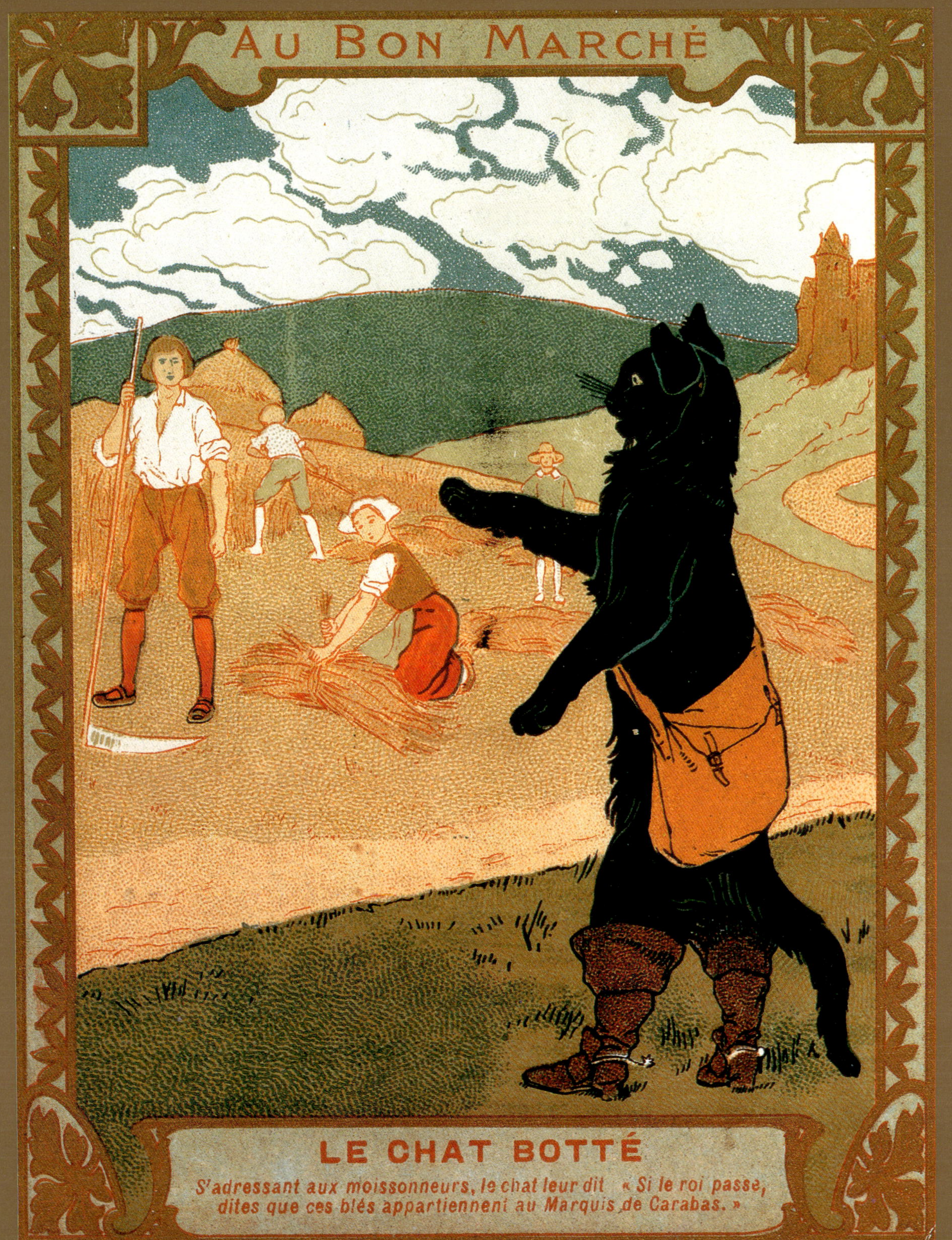
AU BON MARCHÉ
LE CHAT BOTTÉ
S'adressant aux moissonneurs, le chat leur dit « Si le roi passe,
dites que ces blés appartiennent au Marquis de Carabas. »

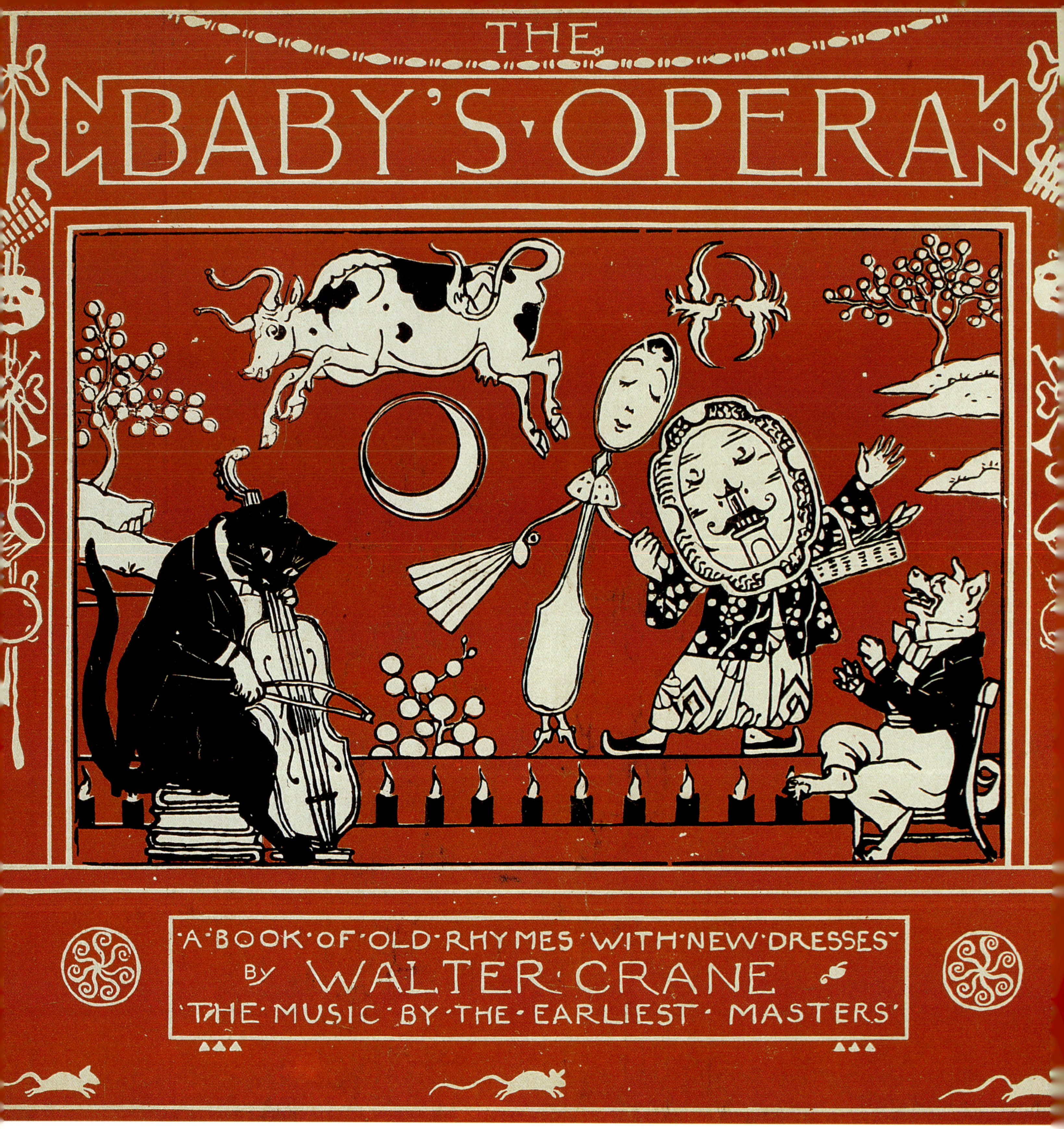

THE

BABY'S·OPERA

·A·BOOK·OF·OLD·RHYMES·WITH·NEW·DRESSES·
BY WALTER·CRANE
·THE·MUSIC·BY·THE·EARLIEST·MASTERS·

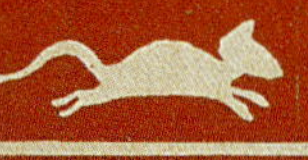

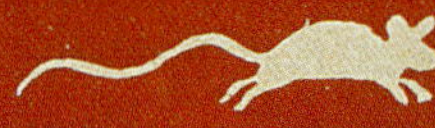

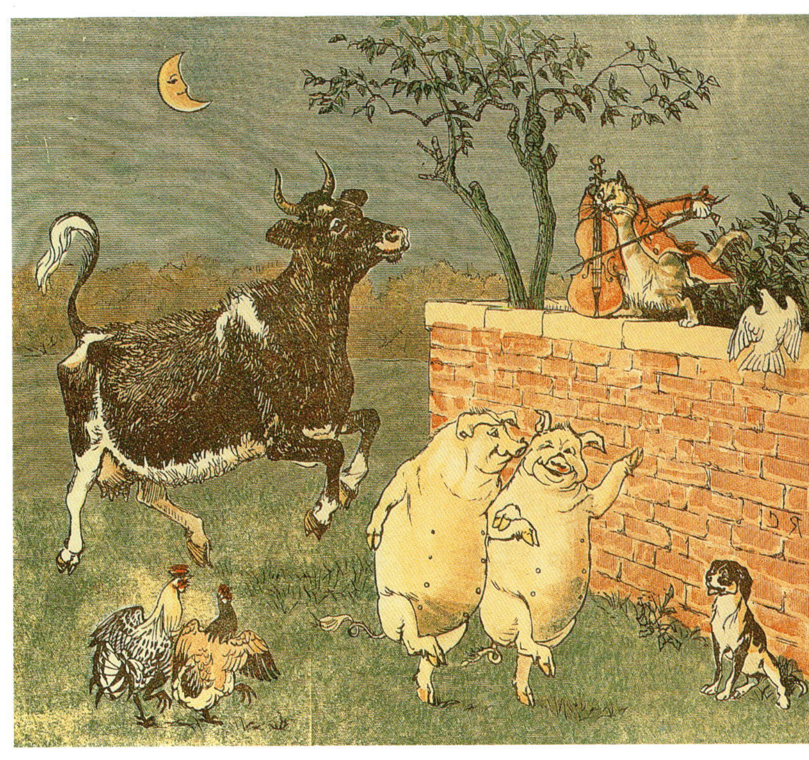

hey diddle diddle
the cat and the fiddle
the cow jumped over the moon
the little dog laughed
to see such fun
and the dish ran away with the spoon

hey diddle diddle

above *Illustrations from* Hey Diddle Diddle *by Randolph Caldecott.*

left *Walter Crane's depiction of the famous nursery rhyme for the cover of his publication,* The Baby's Opera.

Acknowledgements

AKG, London 16, 16-17 tracing, 22-23 left, 23 Top Right, 23 Centre Right, 76, 82-83, 86-87, 88 Background, 89, 90, /©ADAGP, Paris and DACS, London 1999 53,/Erich Lessing 40-41

Bridgeman Art Library, London/New York/©Roger Hilton. 1999 All Rights Reserved, DACS 91, /J & S Antiques, London Front Cover, Back Cover, /Bonhams, London 48-49, 48-49 tracing, /British Library, London 32, /British Museum, London 44-45, /Chris Beetles Ltd, London 45 right, /City of Bristol Museum & Art Gallery ©Peter Blake. 1999 All Rights Reserved, DACS 30, /Fine-Lines (Fine Art), Warwickshire 38-39, /Fleur De Lys Gallery, London 50 Background, 51, /Johannesburg Art Gallery 4, /Kunsthistorisches Museum, Vienna 74-75, /Laing Art Gallery, Newcastle-Upon-Tyne, 66, /Lauros-Giraudon 42, /Louvre Paris 8 right, /Mallett & Son Antiques Ltd, London 1, 1 tracing, 54-55, 64, /Mallett Gallery, London 36, 37, /Musee Fragonard, GrasseLauros-Giradon 59, /Phillips, The International Fine Art Auctioneers, 20-21, /Prado, Madrid 14-15, /Private Collections 32-33 tracing, 33, 46, 62-63, 73, 84-85, 95, /Private Collection/Gavin Graham Gallery, London, UK 43, /Stapleton Collection 92, /The De Morgan Foundation, London 79/Towneley Hall Art Gallery & Museum, Burnley 6-7, 8-9 Background, /Victoria & Albert Museum, London 34, 35 Background

Christie's Images 47, 56, 57 right, 64-65 tracing, 65, 70-71

Corbis UK Ltd/Bettmann 52, 60, /Francis G. Mayer 26, 27, /Seattle Public Library 94

E.T. Archive 28 Background, 29, 35 Top Right, 68 Background, 69, 80, 80-81 tracing, 82 Top Left, 93, /B.W. Robinson 13, /Erika Bruce Collection 25, /Musee du Louvre Paris 10, 11 Background

Mary Evans Picture Library 31 Top, 31 Centre

Sotheby's Picture Library 18-19